At Issue

| The Deep State

Other Books in the At Issue Series

At Issue

| The Deep State

Rita Santos, Book Editor

GREENHAVEN
PUBLISHING

Published in 2019 by Greenhaven Publishing, LLC
353 3rd Avenue, Suite 255, New York, NY 10010

Articles in Greenhaven Publishing anthologies are often edited for length to meet page
requirements. In addition, original titles of these works are changed to clearly present
the main thesis and to explicitly indicate the author's opinion. Every effort is made to
ensure that Greenhaven Publishing accurately reflects the original intent of the authors.
Every effort has been made to trace the owners of the copyrighted material.

Cover image: Colin Dewar/Shutterstock.com

Cataloging-in-Publication Data

Names: Santos, Rita, editor.
Title: The deep state / edited by Rita Santos.
Description: New York : Greenhaven Publishing, 2019. | Series: At issue | Includes
  bibliographical references and index. | Audience: Grades 9–12.
Identifiers: LCCN ISBN 9781534503199 (library bound) | ISBN 9781534503205 (pbk.)
Subjects: LCSH: Political culture—United States. | Power (Social sciences)—Political
  aspects—United States. | Business and politics—United States. | United States—
  Politics and government—21st century. | Conspiracy theories—Social aspects.
Classification: LCC JK1726.D444 2019 | DDC 320.973—dc23

Manufactured in the United States of America

Website: http://greenhavenpublishing.com

Contents

Introduction

The abnormal 2016 election cycle introduced average Americans to the term "deep state," previously used only by conspiracy theorists and those that studied Eastern European politics in the years following World War II (1939–1945). After 2016, "deep state" became part of everyday conversations with little historical context. In 2017, conservative radio pundit Rush Limbaugh proclaimed, "There is already a silent coup, and it's been underway for quite a while to get rid of Donald Trump. And it features a lot of buddies of Brennan, Obama administration holdovers and embeds in the deep state at the Pentagon, State Department, various intelligence agencies."[1] While people outside of Limbaugh's fan base saw these claims as baseless conspiracy theories, his listeners took the idea that civil servants were conspiring against the president as fact. In April 2017, ABC News reported that nearly half of all Americans believed in some kind of a deep state.[2] But what exactly did these people believe?

After the 2016 US presidential election, many began to use the term "deep state" to describe a portion of the government that is not chosen through civilian elections. While elected government officials may get the most press, there are thousands of civil servants who handle the day-to-day activities in each branch of government. A viewpoint by Charles P. Blair and Rebecca L. Earnhardt will explain how these unelected workers help make decisions and carry out the steps needed to keep the government running. Without them, social security checks wouldn't be mailed to seniors, national parks would fall into disrepair, and thousands of other government-run programs would shut down. Some people refer to this type of bureaucracy that continues regardless of who is in public office as the "deep state."

Some fear that these civil servants could use their knowledge of how the government works to further their own political agendas. However, a plan like that would rely on an unignorably large portion of civil servants all secretly having the same beliefs and goals to work. While civil servants likely do have their own opinions about how their departments should be run, this is not a sign of a shadow government. The fact that civil servants aren't elected doesn't mean they can't be fired if they aren't performing their jobs correctly or in accordance with the law. But even within America, the term "deep state" isn't just applied to rogue civil servants. Understanding the historical context of the phrase can help readers understand what the deep state means in countries like Turkey and Pakistan, as well as in America.

Viewpoints by John Light, Shane Ralston, and others will give readers insight into the complicated history of the term "deep state." Originating from the Turkish phrase *derin devlet*, it describes an alleged shadow government that runs what is known as a "state within a state." It is a term for corrupt government or military officials who use their connections to facilitate criminal activity. The Turkish *derin devlet* is believed to be behind that government's inefficacy at curtailing drug running in the 1990s, despite officially condemning it. It is even believed that the Turkish mob worked with certain politicians and law enforcement officials, motivating this inaction. Government corruption at all levels is widespread in countries like Turkey, Egypt, and Pakistan.

As people attempted to make sense of the seismic shift in American politics, some began to make connections that were simply incorrect. These conspiracy theories can be confusing because they often mix facts with fiction. On July 26, 2017, President Trump tweeted that transgender people would no longer be accepted or allowed in the armed services. With the fate of over 15,000 trans service members in their hands, the joint chiefs of staff chose to take no action. People like Rush Limbaugh saw this as proof of the military intentionally disregarding the president's orders as part of a larger deep state conspiracy. While it is tempting to see the military's lack of response as a sign of a deep state on the rise or patriotic rebellion, the truth is far less sensational. As

Marine General Joe Dunford, the chairman of the joint chiefs of staff, explained, "There will be no modifications to the current policy until the President's direction has been received by the Secretary of Defense and the Secretary has issued implementation guidance."[3] President Trump had not actually issued an order to the military, he had simply posted a tweet. The military does not take orders from an easily breeched public platform like Twitter. When the president eventually did attempt to officially order the military to act in August 2017, an injunction was immediately filed on behalf of a group of trans service people. President Trump's tweets had made them aware of their need for legal protection months in advance and allowed them to prepare. What looks like a deep state conspiracy to some is really the work of informed citizens protecting their rights.

Separating fact from fiction when it comes to the deep state can be confusing because of the different meanings of the term. When learning about the deep state, readers must make sure to ask themselves which definition of the term their source is using. As the following viewpoints will show, explaining and proving the existence of the deep state is no easy task. In some ways, what is perceived as deep state activity is actually beneficial to a healthy democracy. Kathryn Flynn will describe how the supposed deep state activity known as whistleblowing attempts to force transparency between government agencies and the American people. Understanding the different meanings of deep state can help us better recognize how democratic governments function and dysfunction.

The viewpoints in *At Issue: The Deep State* offer a diverse array of perspectives on whether the deep state exists and, if so, what it involves. Viewpoint authors will explain how the various members of the federal government fit together, elucidating the relationship between elected politicians, unelected civil servants, and members of the military and intelligence community so that readers can better decide for themselves whether a deep state exists within the US government. This volume will also explain how

conspiracy theories—such as those surrounding the deep state—
form, teaching readers how to identify and deconstruct them.

Notes

1. Limbaugh, Rush. "Communist Obama CIA Director Calls for Coup." *The Rush Limbaugh Show*, July 2017. https://www.rushlimbaugh.com/daily/2017/07/25 /trump-feeds-uncontrolled-beltway-rage-obamas-cia-director-talks-not-so-silent -coup/.

2. Langer, Gary. "Nearly Half of Americans Think There's a 'Deep State': Poll." ABC News, April 27, 2017.

3. Hennigan, W. J. "Top U.S. General Says Pentagon Will Not Change Policy on Transgender Troops Until White House Acts." *L.A. Times*, July 27, 2017. www.latimes .com/politics/washington/la-na-essential-washington-updates-top-u-s-general-tells -military-leaders-1501171360-htmlstory.html.

1

The Historical Context for the Term "Deep State" Is Necessary to Understand It

John Light

John Light is a reporter and digital producer for the Bill Moyers team. His work has appeared in the Atlantic *and* Mother Jones *and on Salon, Grist, Slate, Vox, and Al Jazeera, and has been broadcast on Public Radio International. He is a graduate of Columbia Graduate School of Journalism.*

The term "deep state" has been around since World War I (1914–1918). It was originally conceived to describe a military coup in Turkey that put Mustafa Ataturk in power. Under his authoritarian regime, the country strived to modernize. The term for Ataturk's regime is known to many as the "derin devlet," which translates to "deep state." It was used to describe Ataturk's "state within a state," but the term also gained popularity in the days after the 2016 American presidential election. However, to many Americans the meaning of the phrase was unclear. In the following viewpoint, John Light explains what President Trump's team meant in using the expression "deep state" as well as the historical context for the term.

As the daily drip of information about possible links between Trump's campaign and Russia trickles on, Democrats, commentators and at least some officials in the US intelligence community, it seems, smell a rat. CNN reported last week that according to sources, "The FBI has information that indicates associates of President Donald Trump communicated with suspected Russian operatives to possibly coordinate the release of information damaging to Hillary Clinton's campaign."

Meanwhile, White House sources continue insisting to reporters that there's no fire behind all the smoke. The true story, they say, is a conspiracy by the so-called "Deep State" to undermine a democratically elected president.

Trump and his team are good at taking terms and twisting their meaning to suit their own ends. "Fake news," for example. Once Trump started using it, the mainstream media, which had been using "fake news" to describe online lies packaged in the guise of honest reporting, largely backed away. "Let's put this tainted term out of its misery," *Washington Post* media columnist Margaret Sullivan wrote.

"Deep State" may meet a similar fate, with some anti-Trump commentators arguing that the term, while appropriate for less democratic governments abroad, has no meaning in the United States, and refers to one of many conspiracy theories that found a home at *InfoWars*, *Breitbart*, and, ultimately, in the president's brain. Yet despite that, the idea of a Deep State is useful when talking about the forces that drive US policy. Here's a look at its history and use today.

How Trump Allies Talk About the "Deep State"

In Trump's world, the "Deep State" is a sub rosa part of the liberal establishment, that crowd resistant to the reality TV star's insurgent candidacy all along, and which ultimately was rebuffed by voters on Election Day. Although Trump has taken the helm of the executive branch, this theory goes, his opponents lurk just below the surface. "We are talking about the emergence of a deep state led by Barack Obama, and that is something that we should prevent," Steve King, the right-wing member of Congress from Iowa and a Trump ally, told the *New York Times*.

Implicit is the idea that the intelligence agencies' investigation into Trump and his campaign's Russia ties are baseless, and that leaks about the investigation to the press are part of an effort to undermine him. "Of course, the deep state exists," Trump ally Newt Gingrich recently told the Associated Press. "There's a permanent state of massive bureaucracies that do whatever they want and set up deliberate leaks to attack the president. This is what the deep state does: They create a lie, spread a lie, fail to check the lie and then deny that they were behind the lie."

The claim that the campaign was surveilled by Obama is also part of this supposed Deep State conspiracy; House Intelligence Committee Chair Devin Nunes fanned the flames last Wednesday when he suggested, based on information shared with him by the administration, that Trump advisers' communications were likely collected during the transition, perhaps by accident. *Breitbart* has even started calling the wiretapping story DeepStateGate.

The Deep State Abroad

Historically, the idea of a Deep State is an import; it has been used for decades abroad to describe any network of entrenched government officials who function independently from elected politicians and work toward their own ends.

One such network cropped up decades ago in Turkey, devoted to opposing communism and protecting by any means necessary the new Turkish Republic that Mustafa Ataturk founded after World War I. In the 1950s, the *derin devlet*—literally, "deep state"—began bumping off its enemies and seeking to confuse and scare the public through "false flag" attacks and engineered riots. The network ultimately was responsible for thousands of deaths.

Another shadowy entity exists in present day Pakistan, where the country's main intelligence agency, Inter-Services Intelligence (ISI), and the military exert considerable control over government, often operating independently of the country's elected leaders and sometimes overthrowing them in military coups. "The vast majority of Pakistanis are effectively disenfranchised by this system," wrote Daniel Markey, senior research professor at Johns Hopkins University's School of Advanced International Studies.

"As far as it is possible to know their views through public opinion polling and interviews, it appears that they perceive the state as generally ineffective, often even predatory, in their daily lives."

America's Deep State

Here in the United States, we have another kind of Deep State, one that Mike Lofgren, a former congressional staffer specializing in intelligence, described in an original essay for our site in 2014.

The Deep State, Lofgren wrote, was not "a secret, conspiratorial cabal; the state within a state is hiding mostly in plain sight, and its operators mainly act in the light of day." It is not a tight-knit group, and has no clear objective. Rather, it is a sprawling network, stretching across the government and into the private sector. "It is a hybrid of national security and law enforcement agencies," Lofgren wrote. "… I also include the Department of the Treasury because of its jurisdiction over financial flows, its enforcement of international sanctions and its organic symbiosis with Wall Street." In Lofgren's definition are echoes of President Dwight Eisenhower's famous farewell address in 1961, in which he implored future presidents to "guard against the acquisition of unwarranted influence, whether sought or unsought, by the military-industrial complex."

But in his Obama-era definition of the Deep State, Lofgren also included "the White House advisers who urged Obama not to impose compensation limits on Wall Street CEOs, the contractor-connected think tank experts who besought us to 'stay the course' in Iraq, the economic gurus who perpetually demonstrate that globalization and deregulation are a blessing that makes us all better off in the long run." These individuals pretend they have no ideology—"their preferred pose is that of the politically neutral technocrat offering well considered advice based on profound expertise."

In short, by Lofgren's conception, the Deep State is maintained by the mid-level number crunchers, analysts, congressional staffers and lawyers—technocrats who build and perpetuate the Washington consensus, leading the country in and out of wars, in and out of trade agreements, into and, if we're lucky, out of recessions, without questioning their own judgment. The 2016 election saw voters rebel against that system, and Donald Trump was the surprising result.

A Deep State Divided and Debated

The 2016 election shook up the Deep State. It's without question that elements within it are concerned about Donald Trump and pushing back against him. The FBI, which may have helped Trump win the election with its last-minute announcement about Clinton's emails, is now investigating him. But some elements of the intelligence agencies may also be the source of stories fanning the flames of Trump's wiretapping theory.

On one hand, public servants at the State Department are chafing at Trump's defunding of diplomacy and object to his repeated attempts to put in place a Muslim travel ban. On the other, elements of Lofgren's Deep State, including Wall Street lawyers and alumni of Silicon Valley companies that help the government surveil citizens, have become part of Trump's administration.

We are in a moment where the intelligence community has tremendous power. Leakers continue to give to the press part, but not all of the story; declassified documents and testimony by agency heads before Congress yield few definitive takeaways.

Some on both the left and right hope the Deep State will take Trump down. But civil libertarians and such journalists as Glenn Greenwald have been imploring the media, Democratic politicians and Washington insiders to make sure that in their enthusiasm to get rid of Trump, they do not give intelligence agencies too long a leash or too much ability to shape the narrative. Once they have it, Greenwald argues, the agencies won't want to let it go.

The Deep State to Come

While the Russia story continues to trickle out, Trump and his minions have gotten to work trying to build their own network of loyal informants across the government, a web that resembles the deep states seen abroad more than anything America has known.

Trump's son-in-law, Jared Kushner, reportedly has taken the reins of foreign policy from the State Department and is running it out of the White House. He's also been tasked with overhauling, and potentially privatizing, elements of the federal bureaucracy from his perch at Donald Trump's side. Meanwhile, Trump has installed hundreds of officials across government to serve as his eyes and ears, rooting out those opposed to his administration and pushing his agenda throughout official agencies.

If Obama's Deep State is perceived by Trump as the enemy, his solution is to build his own Deep State to counter it.

2

The Military Industrial Complex Has Become the American Deep State

Shane Ralston

Shane Ralston is an associate professor of philosophy at Penn State University–Hazleton.

While the term "deep state" conjures images of a vast conspiracy, in this viewpoint, professor Shane Ralston cautions that government leaks point to signs of its existence in the United States. It is important that citizens understand how the deep state functions in their country. Leaks can act as a way to check those in power, but they can also be used by the military or CIA to forward the agenda of unelected officials. Ralston points out how the military industrial complex does, in fact, have the power to influence government officials. Here, Ralston addresses the danger of a military coup in the United States.

The notion of the "deep state" or a "state within a state" is creepy, to say the least. It indicates the existence of a shadowy group of unelected bureaucrats deeply embedded in the military-intelligence establishment secretly manipulating government policy.

Ryan McMaken of the Mises Institute defines the "deep state" as "nothing more than agencies and individuals within the US government that have their own interests and their own agendas." McMaken continues:

"Why We Should Fear the Deep State," by Shane Ralston, Intellectual Takeout, March 8, 2017. Reprinted by permission.

> Only the most naïve observers of any government would deny that life-long entrenched bureaucrats don't have their own interests separate from both the public and the public figures who … are subject to public oversight and to elections.

International relations scholars and public administration experts associate deep states with authoritarian regimes, such as Egypt, Turkey, Pakistan and pre-civil-war Syria. However, as we're finding out, the US has its own deep state. While some media outlets portray deep state talk as tantamount to conspiracy theory, the deep state is quite real.

Rumors are swirling that deep state forces are at work undermining Donald Trump's presidency. Are these mere rumors? Quite possibly. But there is also evidence to consider:

Exhibit A: The flow of relatively high-level leaks signals that someone other than the president controls the levers of power in the US government. Amanda Taub and Max Fisher of the *New York Times* report: "Though leaks can be a normal and healthy check on a president's power, what's happening now … risks developing an entrenched culture of conflict between the president and his own bureaucracy."

Exhibit B: The CIA backed Hillary Rodham Clinton's candidacy for president. It then relied heavily on circumstantial evidence to support its allegations that Russia colluded with the Trump campaign to dictate the election's outcome. Journalist Glenn Greenwald, a champion of the left, warned that "cheering *for the CIA* and its shadowy allies to unilaterally subvert the US election and impose its own policy dictates on the elected president is both warped and self-destructive."

Exhibit C: National Security Advisor and retired US Army Lieutenant General Michael Flynn lied to or misled Vice President Mike Pence regarding the substance of talks he had with Russian ambassador Sergey Ivanovich Kislyak. There are suspicions that Flynn's ouster was a "political assassination" by US intelligence.

Exhibit D: President Trump alleges that bureaucrats loyal to the Obama administration, many of whom still hold positions in the administrative state, wire-tapped Trump Tower prior to the election. There are reasons to believe the surveillance occurred, though there is no evidence that the surveillance was politically motivated.

Why should any of this worry regular Americans?

In order to fully appreciate the deep state and the threat it poses to democracy, it's necessary to first grasp the notion of civil-military relations. Professor Patricia Shields of Texas State University summarizes the concept:

> Civil-military relations (CMR) deals with the myriad of policy and administration issues that arise as civilian and military sectors negotiate their place in society and on the world stage. […] For example, CMR may involve an analysis of interactions between presidents and their military advisors, how the defense bureaucracy balances civil and military interactions, the role of culture in military organizations, methods used to recruit soldiers and private contractors work together in counterinsurgency situations and gaps in policy preferences among citizens and soldiers.

Of course, in our democracy, the military is subordinated to civilian control. The president, though a civilian, is also the commander-in-chief of the armed forces. However, as Shields notes, once the military becomes sufficiently strong to defeat civilian militia, a paradox emerges: "Paradoxically, an effective military is then strong enough to threaten the polity itself. This paradox known as the 'civil-military problematique' is at the heart of CMR theory and practice."

The threat is that when the policy preferences of unelected administrators in the military-intelligence bureaucracy diverge from those of elected leaders, the bureaucrats can choose not to carry out the orders of its civilian bosses. (For those who are still skeptical, Shields notes that "the armed forces sidestepped Clinton's campaign promise to fully integrate gays into the military with virtually no consequence.")

When members of the military-intelligence establishment continually disobey civilian leaders (leak information, subvert elections, ignore official policy directives, etc.), civil-military relations break down. The democratic state is put at risk of becoming a so-called banana republic, subject to military coups, or a deep-state controlled autocratic state, similar to Turkey and Egypt, wherein former military and intelligence officers pressure a weak government to carry out their agenda.

So who's afraid of the deep state? I am.

3

The Deep State Is Not a Conspiracy, but It Does Exist

Thomas L. Knapp

Thomas L. Knapp is the director and senior news analyst at the William Lloyd Garrison Center for Libertarian Advocacy Journalism (thegarrisoncenter.org). He lives and works in north central Florida.

Thomas L. Knapp tackles the notion that the deep state is responsible for policy issues faced by the Trump administration. He acknowledges that civil servants—like any individual involved in politics—do what they can to maximize their roles in government and promote their own goals. However, Knapp ultimately asserts that this is merely the nature of politics and that it is not indicative of a vast conspiracy or political corruption. It is simply the fact that unelected workers tend to have the same goal of maximizing their influence that binds them together as "conspirators" in the deep state.

Buzzwords come and buzzwords go. Lately, a trending buzzword—or, I guess, buzz phrase—among the politically inclined is "Deep State." Google News returns 127,000 recent media uses of the phrase.

Every time US president Donald Trump finds himself under attack or just stymied in one of his policy initiatives, his supporters blame the Deep State. The Deep State is behind the "Russiagate" probes. The Deep State doesn't like his Muslim travel ban or his

"What the Deep State Is," by Thomas L. Knapp, William Lloyd Garrison, June 27, 2017.

ObamaCare replacement bill. The Deep State keeps forcing him to break his campaign promises of a less misadventurous US foreign policy. I'm expecting reports, any day now, that the Deep State stole his limo keys and left the toilet seats up in the residence area of the White House.

So what, precisely, is the Deep State? There's actually both more and less to it than you might think.

In a recent Bloomberg column, former Obama administration regulatory czar Cass Sunstein defines the Deep State as merely "the talented professionals who serve both Democratic and Republican administrations, and who are civil servants rather than political appointees." While not incorrect as such, that definition is superficial and not especially informative.

Others identify the Deep State as residing completely or nearly completely in the US "intelligence community" specifically and the Military-Industrial Complex in general, or in Washington's sprawling regulatory apparatus.

It's in the intel/military definition that the idea tends to take on more active, sinister connotations: Spies and generals conspiring to put over a coup of some sort, if necessary maybe even giving inconvenient political figures the JFK treatment. Without discounting that possibility, let me propose that while individuals acting in knowing concert might be a minor feature of the Deep State, they aren't its essence.

In high school civics class theory, elections are meaningful and political government is a highly developed, well-oiled, deliberative decision-making machine in which ideas matter and the best ones win out, to the benefit of all.

In fact, it is in the nature of political government to put its own needs first, and its corps of unelected workers (greatly outnumbering the politicians who have to explain themselves to voters) closely identify its needs with their needs and vice versa.

The aggregate actions of long-term state functionaries will always tend to maximize the state's growth and their own discretionary power. Not because they are venal or corrupt (although some certainly are), nor because they necessarily subscribe to some particular ideology (although some certainly do), but because like their actions, they themselves are an aggregate whose parts will overwhelmingly respond to the same incentives in the same ways.

You'll never walk into a hotel and see a sign in the lobby announcing "Welcome Deep State, Conference Room 3A." The Deep State isn't a conscious conspiracy, even if there are conscious conspirators within it. The Deep State is a large mass with no guiding intellect. Its inertia tends to hold it in one place and/or to carry most of its members in the same direction.

4

Separating Fact from Fiction in Deep State Conspiracy Theories

Charles P. Blair and Rebecca L. Earnhardt

Charles P. Blair is a Washington, DC–based university instructor, researcher, and writer specializing in terrorism and the history, technical underpinnings, and potential futures of weapons of mass destruction and other disruptive technologies.

Rebecca L. Earnhardt is working toward a master's degree in biodefense at George Mason University, with a concentration in terrorism and homeland security. She earned two bachelor's degrees— one in political science and one in homeland security and emergency management—from Virginia Commonwealth University.

With nearly half of Americans believing in some form of the deep state, authors Charles P. Blair and Rebecca L. Earnhardt attempt to explain precisely what Americans should be worried about. This viewpoint seeks to separate fact from conspiracy theory. The authors detail not only the historical roots of the term but also the many conspiracy theories that have followed it through the years. Understanding which version of the deep state people believe in can help foster a more complete understanding in public discourse.

P resident Donald Trump's recent military action against the Syrian government is just the latest instance in which the White House has failed to adhere to policies beloved by the

"Has the Deep State Hoodwinked Trump?" by Charles P. Blair, Rebecca L. Earnhardt, Bulletin of the Atomic Scientists, May 2, 2017. Reprinted by permission.

far right. Though many of the administration's more centrist supporters cheered the US missile strike on the Syrian air base, characterizing it as a bold move necessitated by the weakness of Barack Obama, other Trump supporters argued that the president had been tricked into a grand mistake.

The notion of a "tricked" Trump presents a number of questions: Who is deceiving the president? For what purpose? Was Trump's about-face on Syria merely the result of a humanitarian-infused bid by his family members to blunt the power of the anti-establishment, nationalist, and anti-globalist faction within the White House? Was Trump the victim of a ruse by the "deep state"—a monolithic alignment of federal power centers so intent on maintaining command that it was willing to derail the new administration by encouraging it to pursue unwise military action? Or was the president misled by an even more ominous version of the deep state: one that subverts legitimate civilian leadership in a bid to recouple the United States to "regime change" and similar globalist policies of militant "humanitarian" interventionism? Could the deep state have gone so far as to conduct a false-flag operation, framing the Assad regime for the April 4 chemical weapons attack in Idlib province?

To be clear, one needn't be a far-right extremist to believe that the deep state in some form exists, or to harbor concerns about it. According to a recent *Washington Post*-ABC News poll, nearly half of Americans now believe in the existence of a deep state—when "deep state" is defined as "military, intelligence, and government officials who try to secretly manipulate government policy." Moreover, more than half of Americans who believe in a deep state see it as a "major problem." But some on the radical fringes of the far right attribute Trump's turn-about to the machinations of a deep state of unparalleled monstrousness—a deep state synonymous with a "new world order" or "Zionist Occupation Government" (ZOG). These are terms used by some extremists to describe an international cabal, possibly satanic in origin and usually Jewish in leadership, that seeks global domination. Typical sentiments about this perceived cabal can be found in publications such as the *Daily Stormer,* the most visited radical-right website in the world. In February, the *Daily Stormer* wrote that "Traitors in the [US] 'Intelligence Community' ... also known as ZOG" are working with "Jew accomplices. ... The only way the people of America can take back control of our government is through Trump taking an iron fist to the criminal network that wishes to retain its rule over some evil globalist mongrel empire."

While such sentiments have animated far-right thinking for more than 70 years, few realize what a clear and present danger this latest incarnation of conspiracism represents. As some on the far right propagate their belief that the mainstream media is deliberately concealing a massive conspiracy to subvert President Trump's leadership, they are armed with exponentially growing numbers of seemingly legitimate news stories that appear to support their view. They are also in a sense armed by growing public perceptions about "fake news"—a majority of Americans now thinks that "mainstream news organizations regularly produce false stories." Then again, Trump himself has often engaged in conspiracism, as when he claimed without evidence that the Obama administration had wiretapped Trump Tower; conspiracism emanating from the Oval Office is a new development in US history. A state of affairs in which unprecedented numbers of Americans have lost faith in traditional arbiters of truth and are unable on their own to distinguish fact from fiction presents a profound threat to social cohesion. But the danger extends even further. If the past is any indication, some extremists on the far right are likely considering violent strategies to counter the threats they perceive. If this supposition is correct, it would be in keeping with long-term trends—much of the time since 9/11, far-right extremists have been responsible for more killings in the United States than have extremists motivated by jihadist ideology. In today's super-charged political environment, there's every reason to suspect that far-right conspiracism will continue erupting into violence.

Deep State, Deep Roots

The term "deep state" is only now receiving widespread attention—but for more than a decade, some have postulated deep-state involvement in a variety of nefarious affairs. The term is often traced to the Turkish phrase *derin devlet* (or "secret state"). The Turkish term was popularized amid the Susurluk affair of the 1990s, a scandal that revealed close ties between Turkey's government and its criminal underworld. Academic usage of the term "deep state" often denotes what political scientist Patrick O'Neil describes as "a set of coercive institutions, actors, and relationships beyond those formally charged with defense, intelligence, and policing." But of likely greater salience to contemporary conceptions of the deep state are the writings of controversial political scientist Peter Dale Scott. In an influential 2007 article, Scott linked "the political assassinations of the 1960s, Watergate, Iran-Contra, and now 9/11 [to] … the deep state, that part of the state which is not publicly accountable, and pursues its goals by means which will not be approved by a public examination."

Preoccupation with a global cabal akin to today's "deep state" has animated American thinking for hundreds of years—dark intrigues involving Jesuits, Freemasons, Illuminati, Communists, and so on. The historian Richard Hofstadter, in a seminal 1964 *Harper's Magazine* article called "The Paranoid Style in American Politics," lucidly traced long-standing belief in an "apparatus of education, religion, the press, and mass media [engaging] in a common effort to paralyze the resistance of loyal American" citizens. "Very often," Hofstadter wrote, "the enemy is held to possess some especially effective source of power: [H]e controls the press; he has unlimited funds; [and] he has a new secret for influencing the mind (brainwashing)." Sound familiar? It certainly sounds familiar to some on today's far-right fringe, who equate the deep state with global plots hatched by the new world order or the "Zionist Occupation Government"—or both.

Rise of the New World Order

Conceptions of a nefarious "new world order" have changed over time; in fact, one of the idea's earliest incarnations was largely perceived as benign. In his 1940 non-fiction book *The New World Order*, H.G. Wells called for the creation of just that, "a new world order." Wells, an ardent socialist, warned that failure to create such a one-world apparatus would risk "an entire and perhaps irreparable social collapse." By the 1950s, conspiratorialists such as Robert W. Welch, cofounder of the John Birch Society, linked "the new order" to political figures such as then-President Eisenhower, whom he called "a willing agent of the communist conspiracy ... part of a broader conspiracy dating back to the 1700s, connected to the Bavarian Illuminati and control by a hidden group of Insiders."

In 1985, the far-right conspiracy-theory pioneer Eustace Mullins—a disciple of the poet Ezra Pound—published an influential book, *The World Order: Our Secret Rulers*. The book explored Mullins's belief that "[i]t has taken centuries of patient effort for the World Order to attain the power it exercises today. Its origins as an international force go back to the Phoenician slave traders." With purported Jewish stratagems as its leitmotif, *The World Order* set the stage for growing use of the term "new world order" in the decades to follow. But it wasn't until President George H.W. Bush's repeated use of the term, in a January 1991 address to the nation and in speeches thereafter, that significant numbers of the far-right fringe began to perceive the existence of a widespread—and quite possibly existential—plot for planetary control. "We have before us," Bush said, "the opportunity to forge for ourselves and for future generations a new world order.... . When we are successful—and we will be—we have a real chance at this new world order, an order in which a credible United Nations can use its peacekeeping role to fulfill the promise and vision of the [United Nations'] founders."

Today, virtually all major elements of the diffuse far-right fringe, when characterizing their opponents, refer in some manner to long-standing conceptions of a new world order. For some anti-abortion extremists, the term refers to centralized efforts to exterminate the white race. For some anti-tax radicals, including the resurgent "sovereign citizens movement," the appellation denotes infiltration and subversion of the US government by an insidious conspiracy that replaces legitimate government with an illegitimate, tyrannical government. Some Christian white supremacists perceive the new world order as satanic in origin. In such cases, Jews may be regarded as the direct offspring of the devil; in league with the Antichrist, they naturally direct the new world order. Some secular white supremacists—as recently explained to the authors of this article by Eugene Gallagher, a noted professor of millennialism and new religions—perceive "a Jewish-led effort to usurp the power and autonomy of a genetically superior white race." Finally, some elements of the far-right militia movement portray themselves as the last bastion of patriotic resistance to powerful, nefarious national or global governmental forces; they are self-appointed survivalist protectors of the US Constitution— well-armed sentries wary of the new world order. For example, less than seven months ago a paramilitary group calling itself the Crusaders was apprehended while in the final stages of plotting a massive attack on a housing complex in Kansas. Meanwhile, one far-right website is directly linked to more than 100 murders.

Alternative Facts: An Origin Story

In the 1990s, these heretofore fringe beliefs in a new world order began an ascent into the mainstream—due in part to increased normalization of other conspiracy milieus. Television shows such as *The X-Files* and *Conspiracy Theory with Jesse Ventura*, movies such as *Men in Black* and *The Matrix*, and New Age movements emphasizing panacea health remedies and the existence of lost ancient civilizations—all these resulted in "sanitized conspiracism."

As Michel Barkun, one of the world's leading experts on conspiracy culture, explained to the authors of this article in an interview, such conspiratorial "motifs [came to be] regarded sympathetically by tens of millions of Americans." Before the 1990s, such ideas existed far outside the mainstream, and separate from one another; by now, such motifs have merged into a mélange of conspiracy-prone cultures across the entire political and social spectrum. Uniting these cultures is belief in what Barkun terms "stigmatized knowledge"—ideas that, though they are discounted by the institutions (such as universities and associations of scientific researchers) that traditionally have differentiated between knowledge and fallacy, are regarded by some individuals as substantiated. An important category of stigmatized knowledge is "suppressed knowledge"—that is, assertions that authoritative bodies ostensibly know to be credible but nonetheless suppress. They suppress these assertions out of fear that public knowledge would have harmful societal consequences or, more to the point, they do so for purely selfish or evil reasons. As Barkun points out in his seminal study *A Culture of Conspiracy: Apocalyptic Visions in Contemporary America*, "stigmatization itself is taken to be evidence of truth—for why else would a belief be stigmatized if not to suppress the truth?" For many individuals who accept *one* conspiracy, traditional authority structures become uniformly suspect, and all stigmatized claims can carry with them an almost axiomatic presumption of validity. This, Barkun writes, "greatly facilitates the flow of such claims through the [conspiratorial] milieu."

This elevated circulation of cross-pollinated conspiratorialism, now manifest in the increasingly normalized views of the fringe far right, has been facilitated not just by television and movies, as discussed above, but also by internet platforms. The institutionalization of conspiracy theories in the 1990s coincided with the growing ubiquity of the World Wide Web. Since then, the exponential growth and perceived authoritativeness of the internet have allowed an explosive increase in communication platforms— alternative, and largely without filters—on a scale unimaginable even a decade ago. The result, Barkun writes, is "conspiracism integrated into culture products widely regarded as innocuous forms of entertainment."

Perhaps nowhere is the merging of increasingly sanitized conspiracies currently more evident than in stipulated links between UFOs and the new world order. In 2014, for example, multiple far-right media outlets seized upon an article in Iran's semi-official *Fars News*. The article, claiming access to a secret report by Russia's Federal Security Services, based on documents leaked by Edward Snowden, highlighted "incontrovertible proof that an alien/extraterrestrial intelligence agenda is driving US domestic and international policy, and has been doing so since at least 1945."

Similarly, some far-right conspiracy adherents often draw attention to news stories from the Kremlin-backed media operation RT. This popular news outlet frequently conducts interviews with specialists who present arguments for the existence of UFOs and allege that aliens and the US military exchange technologies. RT's website is host to at least one columnist who specializes in exposing the role that secret societies, such as the Illuminati, allegedly play in directing world affairs. When UFOs, the Illuminati, and new world order conspiratorialism become linked to claims of secret government knowledge—claims based on seemingly legitimate news sources—one sees how suppressed knowledge is formulated, fused, normalized, and widely assimilated into mainstreamed conspiracism. It should come as little surprise, at least when considered in hindsight, that belief in an acutely diabolical deep state has become widespread.

Architecture of Belief

It bears emphasizing that only a minority of the far-right fringe equates the deep state with visions of a truly totalitarian global cabal (though the number of individuals with such beliefs may be growing). Also deserving emphasis is the reality that subsequent findings sometimes validate previously discounted conspiracies. That is, some conspiracies are real—for instance, the CIA at one time administered LSD to unsuspecting American citizens. Indeed, one-time CIA counterintelligence chief James Jesus Angleton is credited with saying, "Deception is a state of mind and the mind of the state."

Today's proliferation of sanitized conspiracies may fuel a shift in the very architecture of belief—what people choose to believe, how they decide to believe it, and how they regard proponents of opposing beliefs. The public's faith in government, science, and the press has steeply declined. Conventional religious authority structures have in many cases dissolved. As Barkun writes, "Traditional forces that might in other circumstances have interfered with the ability of new belief systems to arise [are proving] unable to do so." However one regards particular conspiracy theories, there is little risk of self-deception in recognizing that the United States has now ventured well into uncharted conspiratorial waters.

5

Is the Military Industrial Complex a Threat or Our Last Line of Defense?

James George Jatras

James George Jatras is an analyst, former US diplomat, and foreign policy adviser to the Senate Republican leadership.

In his farewell address to the nation, President Eisenhower warned Americans of the threat of a military industrial complex. Former US diplomat James George Jatras explains how the military industrial complex (MIC) came to power during the Cold War and how that power has continued to grow since then. This is illustrated by the fact that the military now takes up 54 percent of the federal government's budget. Jatras suggests that the American deep state truly came into being when the tactics used to fight the Soviet Union began to be used on American citizens. But he also points out how the MIC could work to protect the country from the president's foreign negotiation fumbles.

As the drumbeat intensifies for what might turn out to be anything but a "splendid little war" against North Korea, it is appropriate to take stock of the ongoing, seemingly successful effort to strip President Donald Trump of his authority to make any foreign and national security policies that fly against the wishes of the so-called Military-Industrial Complex, or MIC. A Google search for "Military Industrial Complex" with "Trump" yields

"If War Comes, Don't Blame the 'Military-Industrial Complex'—Things Are Even Worse Than You Think," by James George Jatras, Strategic Culture Foundation, August 12, 2017.

almost 450,000 hits from all sources and almost 26,000 from just news sources.

During the 2016 campaign and into the initial weeks of his administration, Trump was sometimes described as a threat to the MIC. But over time, with the appointment to his administration of more generals and establishment figures (including some allegedly tied to George Soros) while purging Trump loyalists, it's no surprise that his policies increasingly seem less a departure from those of previous administrations than a continuation of them (for example, welcoming Montenegro into NATO). Some now say that Trump is the MIC's best friend and maybe always was.

There are those who deny that the MIC exists at all. One self-described conservative blogger writing in the pro-war, pro-intervention, and mostly neoconservative *National Review* refers to the very existence of the MIC as a "myth" peddled by the "conspiracy-minded." Sure, it is conceded, it was appropriate to refer to such a concept back when President Dwight Eisenhower warned against it in 1961 upon his impending departure from the White House, because back then the military consumed some 10 percent of the American GDP. But now, when the percentage is nominally just 3.2 percent, less than $600 billion per year, the term supposedly is inapplicable. (There are those who argue that the real cost annually is over $1 trillion, but why quibble.)

There is a germ of truth contained in the reference to money. Compared to the "wars of choice" that have characterized US global behavior since the end of the Cold War with the Soviet Union, the MIC of the 1950s and 1960s was relatively less likely to embark upon foreign military escapades. The existence of a world-class nuclear-armed foe in the form of the USSR moderated tendencies toward adventurism. The most serious "combat" the classic MIC preferred to engage in was inter-service battles for budgetary bounty. Reportedly, once General Curtis LeMay, head of the Air Force's Strategic Air Command, was briefed by a junior officer who repeatedly referred to the USSR as "the enemy." LeMay supposedly interrupted to correct him: "Young man, the Soviet Union is our adversary. Our enemy is the Navy."

But today the "Military-Industrial Complex" is an archaic term that doesn't begin to describe the complexity and influence of current structures. Indeed, even in Eisenhower's day the MIC was more than a simple duplex consisting of the Pentagon and military contractors but also included an essential third leg: the Congressional committees that provide the money constituting the MIC's lifeblood. (Reportedly, an earlier draft of the speech used the term "military-industrial-Congressional" complex, a fuller description of what has come to be called the "Iron Triangle." Asked about the omission from the final text, Eisenhower is said to have answered: "It was more than enough to take on the military and private industry. I couldn't take on the Congress as well.")

Not only did the Iron Triangle continue to expand during the Cold War, when production of military hardware established itself as the money-making nucleus of the MIC, it swelled to even greater proportions after the designated enemy, the USSR, went out of business in 1991. While for one brief shining moment there was naïve discussion of a "Peace Dividend" that would provide relief for American taxpayers from whose shoulders the burden of a "long twilight struggle" against communism (in John Kennedy's phrase) had been lifted, that notion faded quickly. Instead, not only did the hard side of the MIC maintain itself—first in Iraq to fight "naked aggression" by Saddam Hussein in Kuwait, then in the Balkans in the 1990s as part of NATO's determination to go "out of area or out of business"—it then branched out into soft areas of control.

In the past quarter century what began as Eisenhower's MIC has become a multifaceted, hybrid entity encompassing an astonishing range and depth in both the public and private sectors. To a large extent, the contours of what former Congressional staffer Mike Lofgren has called the "Deep State" (which largely through Lofgren's efforts has since become a household word) are those of the incestuous "expert" community that dominates mainstream media thinking but extend beyond it to include elements of all three branches of the US government, private business (especially the financial industry, government contractors, information technology), think tanks, NGOs (many of which are anything but "nongovernmental" but are funded by US official agencies and those of our "allies," satellites, and clients), higher education (especially the recipients of massive research grants from the Department of Defense), and the two political parties and their campaign operatives, plus the multitude of lobbyists, campaign consultants, pollsters, spin doctors, media wizards, lawyers, and other functionaries.

Comparing the MIC of 1961 to its descendant, the Deep State of today, is like comparing a horse and buggy to a Formula One racecar. The Deep State's principals enjoy power and privileges that would have brought a blush to the cheeks of members of the old Soviet *nomenklatura*, of which it is reminiscent.

Indeed, the Deep State's creepy resemblance to its late Soviet counterpart is manifest in its budding venture into the realm of seeking to brand domestic American dissent as treason, to the hearty approval of the loony Left. As described by Daniel McAdams of the Ron Paul Institute for Peace and Prosperity:

> The government would never compile, analyze, and target private news outlets just because they deviate from the official neocon Washington line.
>
> Perhaps not yet. But some US government funded "non-governmental" organizations are already doing just that.
>
> The German Marshall Fund has less to do with Germany these days than it did when founded after WWII as a show of appreciation for the US Marshall Fund. These days it's mostly funded by the US government, allied governments (especially in the Russia-hating Baltics), neocon grant-making foundations, and the military-industrial complex. Through its strangely Soviet-sounding "Alliance for Securing Democracy" project it has launched something called "Hamilton 68: A New Tool to Track Russian Disinformation on Twitter."

This project monitors 600 Twitter accounts that the German Marshall Fund claims are accounts that are involved in promoting Russian influence and disinformation goals. Which accounts does this monitor? It won't tell us. How does it choose which ones to monitor? It won't tell us. To what end? Frighteningly, it won't tell us.'

How ironic that something called the German Marshall Fund is bringing Stasi-like tactics to silence alternative media and opinions in the United States!

The Soviet *nomenklatura* gave up without a fight. It's unlikely its American counterpart will. Whether Trump in the end decides to fight or to seek accommodation is still under debate. Some suggest that by signing the recent bill imposing sanctions on Russia, Iran, and North Korea, he has already surrendered. But either way, war or not, things are going to get very rocky.

6

The Deep State Conspiracy Theories Surrounding President Kennedy's Death

Andrew Kreig

Andrew Kreig is a public affairs commentator, author, attorney, and legal reformer with decades of experience in cutting-edge public policy issues. He is involved with the Justice Integrity Project, a nonpartisan legal reform group, and Eagle View Capital Strategies, a public affairs consultancy he leads. He is based in Washington, DC.

This excerpted article presents an example of the ways in which details are blurred to create conspiracy theories. Author Andrew Kreig describes a theory of historical events in which CIA operatives have the power to murder presidents. He accomplishes this through presenting an in-depth look at the popular deep state conspiracy theory that the CIA assassinated President Kennedy. It was well known that Kennedy opposed using American military power to overthrow the Cuban communist government, and Kreig posits that Kennedy's efforts for peace ultimately led to his assassination.

R ogue US officials conspired with their powerful patrons to assassinate President John F. Kennedy in 1963 primarily because of his opposition to a CIA-led U.S. military overthrow of Cuba's Communist government.

That was a dominant—albeit not universal—theme by speakers at "The National Security State and JFK" conference on June 3 in

"Experts: Deep State Killed JFK For His Cuba Policy, Peace Advocacy," Citizens Against Political Assassinations (CAPA). Reprinted by permission.

a Northern Virginia community that is heavily populated by intelligence, military and other federal workers and retirees.

The forum remains timely for many reasons, including reported Trump plans to renew reprisals against Cuba this week on human rights grounds.

Also, several columns published in recent days by Trump supporters from across the political spectrum, as well as some from within the intelligence community, argue that a Deep State that had targeted both Kennedy and President Nixon over their foreign policies seeks also to end Trump's presidency prematurely.

Regarding the forum:

"The legend constructed around the assassination was clearly a pretext for a Cuban invasion," military historian Douglas Horne told the audience after he retraced many covert steps by intelligence and military leaders to plan invasions of Cuba that Kennedy repeatedly rebuffed. "Although Kennedy's assassination did not trigger an invasion of Cuba it may have been intended to."

Among others endorsing Horne's view on the 11-speaker program was Jacob Hornberger, an attorney, Horne's publisher (including of *JFK's War with the National Security Establishment: Why Kennedy Was Assassinated*), and also the organizer of the conference as president of the Future of Freedom Foundation, which advocates libertarian policies.

"Ever since researchers and commentators began questioning the conclusions of the Warren Report on the assassination of President John F. Kennedy," Hornberger wrote in the foreword to *JFK's War*, "the response has been: Why would the US national-security establishment—that is, the military and the CIA—kill Kennedy?"

The answer, continued Hornberger, "is because Kennedy's ideas about foreign-policy collided with those of the US national-security establishment during the height of the Cold War."

Last weekend was the anniversary of Kennedy's famed "peace speech" on June 10 in 1963 at American University.

As an alternative to conventional wisdom in the mainstream media, some commentators argue that the Kennedy, Nixon and

Trump efforts to achieve better relations with the Soviet Union/ Russia prompted reprisals from a largely unaccountable US Deep State. Historian and former diplomat Peter Dale Scott decades ago began popularizing the term as describing unaccountable government officials, some of whom are CIA loyalists operating under official cover, and their powerful private sector patrons from the fields of banking, munitions, and other global sectors.

[...]

In other words, continued examination of the Kennedy death provides vital perspective about similar patterns affecting current events and commentary, including those regarding Trump foreign policy regarding Cuba and Russia and extending to investigations of the Trump administration by Congress and Special Counsel Robert Mueller.

[...]

Trained to Kill

Former Cuban exile leader Antonio Veciana, author of a recent memoir *Trained to Kill* with Carlos Harrison, is another non-participant in the June 3 forum worth noting before we summarize a chronology provided by these Warren Commission critics.

Veciana, leader of the anti-Castro group Alpha 66 that planned anti-Castro bombings and assassinations in the 1960s, wrote in his memoir published this spring that he and other exiles hated Kennedy for not opposing Castro more forcefully and wanted him dead, much like they wanted Castro murdered.

Veciana, a former high-ranking accountant in pre-Castro Cuba who knew the future leader beginning in their university days, also wrote that he tried to kill Castro more than once in close coordination with the CIA. Veciana wrote also that he once met his CIA handler and friend, David Phillips, along with Oswald in a Dallas office building six weeks before the Kennedy assassination and Oswald's arrest.

Some skeptical scholars have noted that Veciana has given contradictory accounts of his meetings through the years.

Defenders cut him slack by noting that many JFK witnesses have faced pressures and died unexpectedly, and that Veciana survived a 1979 ambush and head-shot wound in Miami during a period when investigators were questioning him.

Veciana says that he believes he owes it to his adopted country, the United States, to provide a record of the past before he dies.

Cuba's Central Role in Kennedy's Assassination

With that background, we synthesize below a chronology cited by a number of the forum speakers pointing to fury against Kennedy by participants in America's so-called Deep State. They were in a position to recruit operatives for assassinations and cover-ups.

Readers can see specifics of June 3 speakers' comments via video recordings of the conference planned by C-SPAN and the Future of Freedom Foundation on their websites. Dates are to be announced.

The background with Cuba appears to be particularly timely. News reports this week such as *Trump Expected To Restrict Trade, Travel With Cuba* on National Public Radio predict that President Trump will announce on Friday in Miami a reversal of President Obama's 2014 restoration of relations. In 2014, the *New York Times* reported Obama's initiative in *US to Restore Full Relations With Cuba, Erasing a Last Trace of Cold War Hostility*.

With that background, we proceed on the chronology distilled from the materials cited above:

Top military and intelligence officials devised a plan during the last months of the Eisenhower administration to overthrow Castro by secretly arming US-assisted Cuban exiles for what became the Bay of Pigs invasion. (The name references a locale with that name.) The task force was led by Vice President Richard Nixon, who was regarded as a hawk on foreign affairs.

President Eisenhower had been commander of Allied Forces in Europe during World War II before his presidency. Eisenhower presided during the 1950s over a massive build-up of the CIA and its paramilitary covert operations under its Director Allen Dulles.

But the Republican president had sought also to end his two terms at a summit meeting with the Soviet Union's premier, another former World War II general who sought via the summit to reduce Cold War tensions and the threat of another world war.

Shortly before the much-anticipated meeting occurred, however, a secret high-altitude "U-2" spy plane flown by CIA pilot Gary Powers operating under military cover crashed in deep in the heart of the Soviet Union. That led to so many embarrassing deceitful comments by Eisenhower and his staff to cover up the spy flight that escalating rhetoric effectively ruined the summit.

Prouty was among those suggesting that a Secret Team, aka Deep State militarists, may have intended that the Powers plane run short of its special hydrogen fuel component in mid-flight so that the overflight might be exposed and thereby disrupt the summit, thereby preserving America's military superiority, which was useful for ongoing covert operations.

Eisenhower nonetheless left office with his now-famous Farewell Address in 1961 warning Americans against a US "Military-Industrial Complex" that threatened the nation's democracy.

Some in military and intelligence circles had supported Kennedy in the 1960 election over Nixon, despite the Republican's hawkish credentials. Some believed the young president, a war hero during World War II and regarded as a firm part of the bipartisan anti-Communist Congress, could be controlled even more than his canny opponent Nixon.

After Kennedy's election he approved a number of hawkish policies. First, he grudgingly approved the Bay of Pigs invasion for March 1961, just two months after he took office, so long as US involvement was hidden and otherwise limited. Kennedy firmly opposed direct, public involvement in such an invasion.

Yet some of Kennedy's most important military and intelligence advisors falsely assumed the young president could be convinced during the crisis to change his mind and approve US reinforcements that were needed to overthrow Castro.

Kennedy stood firm against deployment. As a result, Castro's forces killed more than 100 of the invading force of some 1,600 exiles and captured the rest.

Kennedy publicly took responsibility for the Bay of Pigs disaster but became infuriated at some of his top military and intelligence advisors. He correctly suspected that some had intentionally misled him about the likelihood of success of the invasion.

In late 1961, Kennedy forced the resignations of CIA Director Allen Dulles and the latter's top two deputies, Richard Bissell and Gen. Charles Cabell. Forcing them out was a momentous decision because they were intimately connected to the nation's most powerful financial and government networks.

To cite two of many examples, Dulles had orchestrated the CIA's brilliant rise to power after decades of global diplomacy, spycrafting and legal work, including a partnership at Sullivan & Cromwell, the favored law firm of the nation's most powerful corporations. Ominously, Cabell's brother Earle was mayor of Dallas.

The Bay of Pigs disaster enraged Cuban exiles and other Cold War hawks against Kennedy. Some, including Veciana, described Kennedy as a traitor and hoped for his death, just as they yearned for Castro's.

During this period, Kennedy acted in many ways like a Cold Warrior, especially in public. He ramped up the 1950s US role in Indochina to a level of 16,000 U.S. military "advisors" in Vietnam operating under CIA leadership disguised, according to Prouty, as regular military.

Separately, the president appointed his brother Robert Kennedy, the attorney general, to lead a covert US plan using the CIA, Cuban exiles and others to assassinate Castro. Mafia leadership was intimately involved with plots to kill Castro, which fostered both covert relationships and deadly secrets.

Kennedy became furious with the hawks, particularly when he saw that advisors were refusing to take "no" for an answer on the question of a US invasion of Cuba. By now, most of the story of the Cuban Missile Crisis is well-known whereby Kennedy negotiated removal of Soviet nuclear missiles. But some hawks at high levels resented what they regarded as a lost opportunity to invade Cuba.

That same year, the US Joint Chiefs of Staff under Chairman Lyman Lemnitzer unanimously approved a mind-boggling plan called Operation Northwoods whereby US forces would create murderous false flag attacks on US private citizens and blame the carnage on Castro, thereby justifying an invasion. Details included an engineered "shootdown" of a drone airliner, riots in Florida, and other murderous events.

Kennedy rejected the plan and forced Lemnitzer out of office. We now know about Operation Northwoods only because Oliver Stone's 1991 movie *JFK* prompted congressional action to declassify vast numbers of Cold War documents via the Assassination Records Review Board.

We know also that Kennedy late in his presidency began issuing highly secret orders that curtailed CIA covert military, spy, assassination and regime change operations. The president also started a process to withdraw US forces from Vietnam after what he hoped would be his 1964 re-election. Some scholars report that he planned to drop Vice President Johnson from the 1964 re-election ticket.

Meanwhile, JFK was becoming increasingly hated by certain powerful forces, including Cuban exiles, segregationists, and organized crime leaders. Some such groups were violence prone and vocal.

But Kennedy also seemed to know that his most dangerous foes might be close to home. That's why he loaned use of the White House for scenes in the 1964 movie *Seven Days In May* (based on a 1962 book) portraying a US military coup against a US president.

Kennedy's famous "peace speech" at American University in 1963 contained what has been widely interpreted as his recognition that his policies put his life in danger: "Our most basic common link is that we all inhabit this small planet," Kennedy told graduates in what scholars regard as a sharp break with his Cold War rhetoric and a possible premonition of a deadly rebellion brewing against his presidency. "We all breathe the same air. We all cherish our children's future. And we are all mortal."

[...]

7

Whistleblowers and Leakers Are a Necessary Power Check for Elected Officials

Kathryn Flynn

Kathryn Flynn completed her PhD at the University of Wollongong. Her interests are in Medicare fraud, public policy, and the media.

Kathryn Flynn explains how transparency in government activities ensures that the will of the people is carried out. When government officials attempt to hide fraud and other types of illegal activities, it is the responsibility of civil servants to act as whistleblowers or leakers, making the public aware of these activities and holding officials accountable for their misdeeds. In this article, she explains the difference between the two and how both can act as checks for those in power. She argues that there is more legal protection for whistleblowers, but leakers often provide more important information to the public. She also discusses what people should consider before choosing to become a leak.

Introduction

In a democracy people need access to information on political, social and economic issues in order to judge whether their elected officials are acting in the public interest. However, too often their elected officials evade such scrutiny and fraud and abuse goes unchecked. Most people with access to relevant information are deterred from leaking or whistleblowing due to legislative prohibitions. They may be those embodied in official secrets acts

"The Practice and Politics of Leaking," by Kathryn Flynn, the University of Wollongong, 2011. Reprinted by permission.

or the case of the United States the Espionage Act (1917). The Official Secrets Act covers legislation providing for the protection of state secrets and official information and is used in the United Kingdom, India, Ireland and Malaysia. Australia does not have an Official Secrets Act but has provisions under Part VII of the Crimes Act (1914) restricting Commonwealth public servants from revealing confidential information. The US Espionage Act has a more limited application. This act only applies to the prohibition on the disclosure of government information on defence issues. While governments have aimed to keep official secrets confidential public servants with access to this material have been successful in releasing it to the public either through the press or in recent times passing it to WikiLeaks, a website for newsworthy leaks.

To draw a distinction between whistleblowing and leaking, whistleblowers are overt in their disclosure of organisational deviance, but there is a price. Bureaucracies now know where their opposition is coming from, and can isolate the whistleblowers by discrediting them, not giving them access to further information and suspending them from work. Generally leakers don't suffer these reprisals.

The definition of leaking is blurred; it can mean an unauthorised source giving information to a journalist but it can also involve an authorised source with political power and high status using the media to their advantage with little likelihood of being prosecuted (Tiffen 1989: 97). In both instances leakers are covert in their disclosure of information. The types of leaker discussed in this article are workers in the public sector who without authorisation convey official information to recipients outside of government (Standing Committee 67). It is usually released to the media in the public interest and these leakers lack positions of high status and power. The information they provide journalists has not been processed by official channels and there is an undertaking by the journalist that the identity of the source will not be revealed. This practice provides some measure of protection to the leaker. Journalists are the usual recipients of leaked information but on occasion information is leaked to activists who can act as a spur to additional media coverage of the story (Martin 2009 206-216). There can be a range of motives for leaking not all of them altruistic. Some leaks are vexatious in nature and not in the public interest. The protection for journalists lies in checking the information with many sources and gauging their reliability (Flynn 2006 264-265).

The examples of leaking discussed in this paper are mainly Australian ones but the issue is applicable to many other countries. Leaks can come from a range of organisations; they may be governments, not-for-profit groups, corporations, environmental groups, trade unions as well as churches. This paper also mainly focuses on leaks from governments.

Not surprisingly governments and unions will not protect leakers if they are caught even when they are acting in the public interest. But there are divergent meanings of the phrase "the public interest." Journalists and leakers define it as information that brings accountability and transparency to government and exposes maladministration or corruption. Governments argue that they are the interpreters of the public interest and that public servants are be bound by rules of confidentiality and are not free to speak out on malfeasance. As Peter Shergold, Secretary of the Department of Prime Minister and Cabinet in the Australian government explained, leaking by public servants is "not just a criminal offence but also democratic sabotage" (Shergold 2004). Supporting this view the then National Secretary of the Community and Public Sector Union, Stephen Jones, giving evidence to the House of Representatives Standing Committee on Legal and Constitutional Affairs in its report on whistleblowing protection, held that leaking should not be protected due to its harmful impact on the relationship between the executive and the public service. Presenting a different perspective to this committee was Peter Bennett, president of Whistleblowers Australia. He argued that the official responses to people who leak confidential information are outrageous and that leakers should be protected from civil and criminal liability (Standing Committee 2009 67).

The Practice of Leaking

One of the difficulties for a public servant who sees evidence of what they perceive is an organisation's corrupt practice and believes that neither management nor parliament will do anything about the problem, is deciding what to do next. They may be influenced by the rhetoric of senior bureaucrats who assert that leaking undermines the trust between the executive and the public service. This might seem a compelling argument except it hides the need for information to be freely available so there is effective decision-making.

- If a leaker decides to speak to a journalist, they must first decide which media outlet is most suitable for publicising the story, whether it is a national or local outlet and what the outlet's editorial policy on the issue is. In selecting a reporter it is recommended to approach one who is experienced and has a reputation for maintaining confidentiality.
- Leakers need to understand the importance of the timing of the release of documents.
- A leaker needs to be armed with documents in order to be believed by a journalist, unless he or she is an experienced and reliable source.
- In addition knowledgeable leakers advise briefing the journalist with a clear and compelling one page summary of the key issues of the case.
- The biggest problem with passing documents across to the media is that photocopiers tend to leave a signature on the copied document, which could be dust or the electronic idiosyncrasies of the machine. So the best way to photocopy the document/s is to use a photocopier in an offsite facility, for example, in a newsagency, library or internet cafe. When the journalist receives the document request him or her to re-photocopy the document and shred the document they had received (which is not the original). It is best to avoid using departmental photocopiers, fax machines,

computers, email or telephones (The Art of Anonymous Activism 2002).

- The print media are preferable to television as print is better able to ensure the leaker's anonymity. Television productions quite often need shadow outs or use distorted voice— and the original voice sometimes can be reconstructed. Television and radio will often do stories inspired by a print story.
- Some leakers, including WikiLeaks founder Julian Assange, believe that leaking is best undertaken by one person working alone who maintains confidentiality. Again others derive safety from working in a group, with information being streamed through a designated spokesperson. In this way the journalist knows the identity of only one of the leakers. Others believe that with group involvement the security of the operation is compromised as someone in the group may drop their guard and talk openly about the leaked information.
- Leaking is unpopular with managers for it is embarrassing and can highlight workplace incompetence, inefficiency and secrecy. The leaker is left in a strong position as his or her identity is hard to uncover and they may be able to stay in the job and leak further information at some stage in the future.
- Reactions by staff members to leaks can be to find the source of the leak and pass further additional information to this source so it gets into the public arena.
- If leakers are caught it can result in the same reprisals that whistleblowers are subject to—demotion or loss of employment and in fact, to find the leakers, managers may resort to targeting innocent people and attributing them with the leak. This can have the desired effect of making the leaker come forward with an admission of guilt.
- There are risks in leaking. The identity of the leaker may be disclosed during the course of a parliamentary inquiry

or by accidental disclosure, for example when a document is passed to a journalist by fax machine.
- On the positive side leaking can influence government policy because it can result in some aspects of public policy being examined more thoroughly than they would in an environment where policy is not subject to such scrutiny (Flynn 2006).
- Further information on methods of leaking can be found in Nicky Hager and Bob Burton's book *Secrets and Lies* (Hager & Burton 1999), a booklet *The Art of Anonymous Activism* (2002) and Julian Assange's article *How a Whistleblower Should Leak Information* (Assange 2010).

Case Study—Medibank

There are many instances where principled public servants have come forward to disclose waste and fraud but one that I am familiar with concerns Medibank—the precursor to Medicare—where whistleblowers and leakers disclosed information to the media, and the Joint Committee of Public Accounts (JCPA) of fraud and abuse against Medibank.

Medibank was a system of publically funded universal health care that was introduced in Australia in 1975. It enjoyed great electoral popularity but there was a defect with the scheme. It had no legislative architecture to control fraud and overservicing, and with few systems in place and inadequate staffing, the Department of Health was left to manage the situation as best it could.

Medibank's first fraud investigator and first whisleblower was Joe Shaw. In 1978 he estimated $100m was being lost to fraud and overservicing and wrote a report outlining his concerns. He was not listened to and he resigned. Some months later, he gave it to a journalist working for Brisbane's *Courier Mail* newspaper. The article was a page one story. Two days later Senator Mal Colston asked that Shaw's report be tabled in parliament. This request was refused. Four years later, committee members of the JCPA recognised the value of Shaw's report. This made it more difficult for senior management in the Department of Health to deny knowledge of the problem.

The second whistleblower was John Kelly, Director of the Operations Branch of the Commonwealth Department of Health. He had been asked by a senior officer of the Department of Health to provide a departmental briefing for the Minister. Kelly's estimate of the amount lost through leakage to the system was the same as Joe Shaw's estimate. Kelly was aware that this information was likely to be deleted by senior management, so using a strategy that was procedurally correct; he hid the estimate in a complicated statistical appendix in an attachment to the brief to the Minister. A senior officer in the Department of Health reading Kelly's report did not grasp the significance of the statistical data and the report was forwarded to the Minister. This figure was then sent to the Australian Medical Association (AMA) who accepted the figure as the amount lost through fraud and overservicing.

It was to be the actions of whistleblowers, leakers, the media, the AMA and the Auditor-General's office in 1981 that led the JCPA to undertake an inquiry into abuse of the Medical Benefits Schedule by medical practitioners.

A freelance journalist, Katherine Beauchamp, was employed by the JCPA from February to September 1982 to prepare questions for the committee. She interviewed whistleblowers, unauthorized confidential sources and high ranking officials. However, her use of material from leakers raised the ire of the Committee and she was suspended from her employment.

The Chairman of the Committee, David Connolly, had received leaked information that either the Victorian division of the Commonwealth Department of Health, or individual staff members of that office, had facilitated criminal fraud by some doctors (JCPA *Report* 203, 1982 48).

Connolly subpoenaed forty-one files from the Commonwealth Department of Health's Melbourne office relating to this matter. On the first day of the Committee's hearings it was announced that there would be no discussion of the forty-one files (JCPA vol. 1,

1 July 1982 303) as the citing of the names of doctors could prejudice police investigation of the trials of those mentioned in the files.

A confidential unauthorised source leaked the police report of the files to Michael Smith, an investigative journalist with Melbourne's *The Age* newspaper, who wrote the story under the headline "Medifraud Cover-Up Suspected." On 13 September 1982 there were further revelations. The story "Medifraud: A Tale of Political Failure" was compiled from leaked government documents and other sources and helped put pressure on the government to complete an interim report earlier than expected. Its publication in December 1982 contained forty-five recommendations and it validated the stance taken by whistleblowers and leakers for government action on medical fraud and overservicing.

In this case study the leaker/s were successful in passing over information to the media in ways that protected their anonymity. Whoever the culprit/s were they were not caught, discredited or suspended from work. They were able to maintain the secrecy of their covert manoeuvre to get information to the media and bypass official channels. The leaker/s took documentary evidence to an experienced journalist who investigated the claims of the leaker/s, collected further evidence and wrote newspaper articles on the topic. The timing of the release of the documents was fortuitous. The editor of the newspaper was interested in white collar crime, the health debate and exposés of policy failures of the Fraser government. This was a government already weakened by scandals and leakers and whistleblowers were emboldened to make disclosures that would be effective (Flynn 2004 218).

The Bigger Picture

Leakers and whistleblowers acted in concert and fought for media and parliamentary oversight of fraud and abuse against Medibank. These acts come under the umbrella of what political theorist John Keane called "monitory democracy." This was a new form of democracy born in the post world war two period which saw the emergence of communicative technologies—the photocopier, the scanner, the fax machine and later the Internet, mobile phones and video recorders. It enabled citizens to more effectively monitor the actions of government and with the help of the media tell others about matters that have been covered up (Keane 2009). Peter Shergold's admonition that leaking was "democratic sabotage" is at odds with monitory democracy: the corrective to unnecessary secrecy and unaccountable power.

One influential monitor on democracy was Daniel Ellsberg, an employee of the Rand Corporation and an advisor to the Pentagon in the 1960s. Initially he was a supporter of the war in Vietnam but in the course of his employment he uncovered evidence that the Johnson administration had lied about its involvement in the war. Ellsberg decided to take action. He photocopied the evidence of the government's deception, a hefty 7,000 page set of documents called the Pentagon Papers and leaked this information to the *New York Times* in 1971 (Ellsberg 2002). There were long legal delays before the *Times* started to publish the documents. The government issued injunctions to prevent publication of any other papers in the series. The matter ended up in the Supreme Court, which ruled against the injunctions and this generated adverse publicity for the government.

When asked whether he would have used this approach today Ellsberg replied that to avoid the legal delays he would have scanned the documents onto the Internet. Julian Assange argued that for someone in Ellsberg's position it would be better to go to a mainstream outlet to get maximum publicity but use WikiLeaks for the storage of the documents. This has the advantage, Assange told the *New York Times*, that the material can be verified in the same way that an academic paper can be verified.

Learning More

Much has changed since the inception of newspaper investigative journalism. In 2006 WikiLeaks was developed as a safe house for newsworthy leaks which are of political, historic or ethical significance. The site is located on servers in Sweden, Belgium and the United States. It maintains its own servers, keeps no logs and uses military grade encryption to protect sources and other confidential information. To date they have not released a misattributed document.

The website has had significant successes. These include the release of the Afghan War Logs, the Iraqi War Logs and US embassy diplomatic cables. The mainstream media picked up these stories on WikiLeaks and the level of publicity, which ensued, encouraged other leaking activists to send material to this site. The retaliatory action taken by the US government was to imprison the alleged leaker Bradley Manning.

Most unauthorised leakers do not meet such a fate. In fact they are successful in reaching their goals. They may be to get information via the media into the public arena, or to expose government policy to wider and more rigorous community debate. Some want to drive a wedge between the executive and the parliament by setting a doubt in the mind of politicians that they are not being well briefed by senior officers of their departments through the omission or cover-up of information. For others it is to achieve more substantial social or political reform than any parliamentary inquiry can achieve.

Julian Assange has a different agenda and a bolder ambition. He is more interested in societies being based on justice rather than on transparency and openness, although these goals can converge. In essays written in 2006 he explained his position. The goal is to "radically shift regime behaviour." He argued,

> We must understand the key generative structure of bad governance...we must use these insights to inspire within us and others a course of ennobling and effective action to replace the structures that lead to bad governance with something better (Assange 2006a).

He likens this bad governance to a conspiracy and by that he means the ability of political elites to hold on to power through the secrecy of their plans and actions which work to the detriment of the population. Conspiracies can be undone by mass leaking. The idea is to increase the porousness of the conspiracy's information system so that the conspiracy will turn against itself in self-defence. As the lines of communication are interrupted the information flow decreases to the point where the conspiracy is not able to govern.

Where this bold ambition leads is yet to be seen but in the meantime whether it is on WikiLeaks or in mainstream journalism leaking provides an alternative to whistleblowing or just doing nothing in the face of corruption, fraud, waste, abuse or hazards to the public. Leakers can be effective in redressing these injustices but they need to be mindful of the precautions to be taken to protect their anonymity.

I wish to thank Jørgen Johansen, Liam Phelan, Brian Martin, William de Maria, Sandrine Therese, Lyn Carson, Colin Salter, Sharon Callaghan and Ian Miles for helpful comments on the draft of this paper.

References

Assange, J. (2006a) *Conspiracy as Governance*, December 3, 2006
URL: http://estaticos.elmundo.es/documentos/2010/12/01/conspiracies.pdf. Consulted 17/12/2010.

Assange, J. (2006b) *State and Terrorist Conspiracies*, November 10, 2006
URL:http://iq.org/conspiracies.pdf. Consulted 17/12/2010.

Assange, J. (2010) *How a Whistleblower Should Leak Information*
URL: http://mathaba.net/news/?x=625093.html. Consulted 11/12/2010.

Australia. Parliament. House of Representatives. (2009). Standing Committee on Legal and Constitutional Affairs. *Whistleblower protection: a comprehensive scheme for the Commonwealth public sector: report of the inquiry into whistleblowing protection within the Australian government public sector*. Canberra.

Ellsberg, D. (2002). *Secrets: A Memoir of Vietnam and the Pentagon Papers*. New York: Viking.

Flynn, K. (2004). *Medical Fraud and Inappropriate Practice in Medibank and Medicare, Australia 1975-1995*, PhD Thesis University of Wollongong.

Flynn, K. (2006). "Covert disclosures: Unauthorized leaking, public officials and the public sphere," *Journalism Studies*, 7(2): 256-273.

Hager, N. and B. Burton (1999). *Secrets and Lies: The Anatomy of an Anti-Environmental PR Campaign*, Nelson, New Zealand: Craig Potton Publishing.

Keane, J. (2009). *The Life and Death of Democracy*. New York: Simon & Schuster.

Martin, B. (2009). "Corruption, outrage and whistleblowing." In eds. Ronald J. Burke and Cary L. Cooper, *Research Companion to Corruption in Organizations* (Cheltenham, UK: Edward Elgar) 206-216.

Project on Government Oversight, Government Accountability Project, Public Employees for Environmental Responsibility (2002), *The Art of Anonymous Activism: Serving the Public while Surviving Public Service Washington, D.C.* URL: http://www.pogo.org /report-corruption. Consulted 9 April 2010.

Shergold, P. (2004). Address to the Australian Graduate School of Management/Harvard Club of Australia held at the National Press Club 17 November 2004 "Plan and Deliver: Avoiding Bureaucratic Hold-up." URL: http://pandora.nla.gov.au/pan/53903/20051109 0000/www.pmc.gov.au/speeches/shergold/plan_and_deliver2004-11- 17.html. Consulted 27 May 2010.

Tiffen, R. (1989) *News and Power*, Sydney: Allen & Unwin.

8

Political Leakers Are Punished More Severely Than Government Criminals

Tom Engelhardt

Tom Engelhardt created and runs the Tomdispatch.com website, a project of the Nation Institute, where he is a fellow. He is the author of a highly praised history of American triumphalism in the Cold War, The End of Victory Culture, *and of a novel,* The Last Days of Publishing, *as well as a collection of his Tomdispatch interviews,* Mission Unaccomplished. *Each spring he serves as a teaching fellow at the Graduate School of Journalism at the University of California–Berkeley.*

Tom Engelhardt suggests that the CIA regularly carries out illegal activities such as kidnapping, torture, and murder with little oversight from the American people. He argues that because the CIA can commit such crimes without facing any sort of judicial censure, it has become a dangerous deep state and a threat to legitimate governance. Engelhardt points out that while CIA officials seem to be above arrest, those that leak government secrets are not. In the past, leakers like Edward Snowden or Chelsea Manning, who have revealed evidence of government crimes, have been punished more severely than the people revealed to have committed the crimes.

"Too Big to Jail? Why Kidnapping, Torture, Assassination, and Perjury Are No Longer Crimes in Washington," by Tom Engelhardt, April 21, 2014. Reprinted by permission.

How the mighty have fallen. Once known as "Obama's favorite general," James Cartwright will soon don a prison uniform and, thanks to a plea deal, spend 13 months behind bars. Involved in setting up the earliest military cyberforce inside US Strategic Command, which he led from 2004 to 2007, Cartwright also played a role in launching the first cyberwar in history—the release of the Stuxnet virus against Iran's nuclear program. A Justice Department investigation found that, in 2012, he leaked information on the development of that virus to David Sanger of the New York Times. The result: a front-page piece revealing its existence, and so the American cyber-campaign against Iran, to the American public. It was considered a serious breach of national security. On Thursday, the retired four-star general stood in front of a US district judge who told him that his "criminal act" was "a very serious one" and had been "committed by a national security expert who lost his moral compass." It was a remarkable ending for a man who nearly reached the heights of Pentagon power, was almost appointed chairman of the Joint Chiefs of Staff, and had the president's ear.

In fact, Gen. James Cartwright has not gone to jail and the above paragraph remains—as yet—a grim Washington fairy tale. There is indeed a Justice Department investigation open against the president's "favorite general" (as Washington scribe to the stars Bob Woodward once labeled him) for the possible leaking of information on that virus to the *New York Times*, but that's all. He remains quite active in private life, holding the Harold Brown Chair in Defense Policy Studies at the Center for Strategic and International Studies, as a consultant to ABC News, and on the board of Raytheon, among other things. He has suffered but a single penalty so far: he was stripped of his security clearance.

A different leaker actually agreed to that plea deal for the 13-month jail term. Nearly three weeks ago, ex-State Department intelligence analyst Stephen E. Kim pled guilty to "an unauthorized disclosure of national defense information." He stood before US District Judge Colleen Kollar-Kotelly, who offered those stern words of admonition, and took responsibility for passing classified information on the North Korean nuclear program to Fox News reporter James Rosen in 2009.

Still, someday Cartwright might prove to be unique in the annals of Obama era jurisprudence—the only Washington figure of any significance in these years to be given a jail sentence for a crime of state. Whatever happens to him, his ongoing case highlights a singular fact: that there is but one crime for which anyone in America's national security state can be held accountable in a court of law, and that's leaking information that might put those in it in a bad light or simply let the American public know something more about what its government is really doing.

If this weren't Washington 2014, but rather George Orwell's novel *1984*, then the sign emblazoned on the front of the Ministry of Truth—"War is Peace, Freedom is Slavery, Ignorance is Strength"—would have to be amended to add a fourth slogan: Knowledge is Crime.

Seven Free Passes for the National Security State

With Cartwright as a possible exception, the members of the national security state, unlike the rest of us, exist in what might be called "post-legal" America. They know that, no matter how heinous the crime, they will not be brought to justice for it. The list of potentially serious criminal acts for which no one has had to take responsibility in a court of law is long, and never tabulated in one place. Consider this, then, an initial run-down on seven of the most obvious crimes and misdemeanors of this era for which no one has been held accountable.

Kidnapping

After 9/11, the CIA got into kidnapping in a big way. At least 136 "terror suspects" and possibly many more (including completely innocent people) were kidnapped off the streets of global cities, as well as from the backlands of the planet, often with the help of local police or intelligence agencies. Fifty-four other countries were enlisted in the enterprise. The prisoners were delivered either into the Bush administration's secret global system of prisons, also known as "black sites," to be detained and mistreated, or they were "rendered" directly into the hands of torturing regimes from Egypt to Uzbekistan. No American involved has been brought to court for such illegal acts (nor did the American government ever offer an apology, no less restitution to anyone it kidnapped, even those who turned out not to be "terror suspects"). One set of CIA agents was, however, indicted in Italy for a kidnapping and rendition to Egypt. Among them was the Agency's Milan station chief Robert Seldon Lady. He had achieved brief notoriety for overseeing a *la dolce vita* version of rendition and later fled the country for the United States. Last year, he was briefly taken into custody in Panama, only to be spirited out of that country and back to safety by the US government.

Torture (and Other Abuses)

Similarly, it will be no news to anyone that, in their infamous "torture memos," officials of the Bush Justice Department freed CIA interrogators to "take the gloves off" and use what were euphemistically called "enhanced interrogation techniques" against offshore prisoners in the Global War on Terror. These "techniques" included "waterboarding," once known as "the water torture," and long accepted even in this country as a form of torture. On coming to office, President Obama rejected these practices, but refused to prosecute those who practiced them. Not a single CIA agent or private contractor involved was ever charged, no less brought to trial, nor was anyone in the Bush Justice Department or the rest of an administration which green-lighted these practices and whose top officials reportedly saw them demonstrated in the White House.

To be accurate, a single member of the national security state has gone to prison thanks to the CIA's torture program. That was John Kiriakou, a former CIA agent who tortured no one, but offended the Obama administrations by turning whistleblower and going public about Agency torture. He is now serving a 30-month prison sentence "for disclosing a covert operative's name to a reporter." In other words, the only crime that could be prosecuted in connection with the Agency's torture campaign was one that threatened to let the American public know more about it.

Now, however, thanks to leaks from the embattled Senate Intelligence Committee's 6,300-page report on the CIA's interrogation and torture program, we know that the Agency "used interrogation methods that weren't approved by the Justice Department or CIA headquarters." In other words, its agents went beyond even those techniques approved in the torture memos, which in turn means that they acted illegally even by the standards of the Bush administration. This should be an obvious signal for the beginning of prosecutions, but—not surprisingly—it looks like the only prosecution on the horizon might be of whoever leaked parts of the unreleased Senate report to McClatchy News.

The Destruction of Evidence of a Crime

To purposely destroy evidence in order to impede a future investigation of possible criminal acts is itself, of course, a crime. We know that such a thing did indeed happen. Jose Rodriguez, Jr., the head of CIA clandestine operations, destroyed 92 videotapes of the repeated waterboardings of Khalid Sheikh Mohammed, who planned the 9/11 attacks, and alleged al-Qaeda operative Abu Zubaydah, "tapes that he had been explicitly told to preserve as part of an official investigation." The Justice Department investigated his act, but never charged him. He has since defended himself in a book, *Hard Measures*, saying that he was, in essence, "tired of waiting for Washington's bureaucracy to make a decision that protected American lives." He is still free and writing op-eds for the *Washington Post* defending the interrogation program whose tapes he destroyed.

The Planning of an Extralegal Prison System

As is now well known, a global network of extralegal prisons, or "black sites," at which acts of torture and abuse of every sort could be committed was set up at the wishes of the highest officials of the Bush administration. This system was created specifically to avoid putting terror suspects into the US legal system. In that sense, it was by definition extralegal, if not illegal. It represented, that is, a concerted effort to avoid any of the constraints or oversight that US law or the US courts might have imposed on the treatment of detainees. This was a well-planned crime committed not under the rubric of war against any specific power, but of a global war without end against al-Qaeda and like-minded groups.

The Killing of Detainees in that Extralegal System

The deaths of detainees in CIA custody in offshore (or borrowed) prisons as a result of harsh treatment ordered by their Agency handlers was not considered a crime. In two cases—in the "Salt Pit" in Afghanistan and at Abu Ghraib prison in Iraq—such deaths were investigated by the Justice Department, but no one was ever charged. In the case of Gul Rahman, the prisoner in the Salt Pit, according to the *Washington Post*, "a CIA officer allegedly ordered Afghan guards in November 2002 to strip Rahman and chain him to the concrete floor of his cell. Temperatures plunged overnight, and Rahman froze to death. Hypothermia was listed as the cause of death and Rahman was buried in an unmarked grave." (In a rare case brought before a military court, a low-level Army interrogator was convicted of "killing an Iraqi general by stuffing him face-first into a sleeping bag," and sentenced to "forfeit $6,000 of his salary over the next four months, receive a formal reprimand, and spend 60 days restricted to his home, office, and church.")

Assassination

Once upon a time, off-the-books assassination was generally a rare act of state and always one that presidents could deny responsibility for. Now, it is part of everyday life in the White House and at the

CIA. The president's role as assassin-in-chief, as the man who quite literally makes the final decision on whom to kill, has been all-but-publicly promoted as a political plus. The drone assassination campaigns in Pakistan, Yemen, and Somalia, though "covert" and run by a civilian agency (with much secret helpfrom the US Air Force) are openly reported on in the media and discussed as a seeming point of pride by those involved. In 2009, for instance, then-CIA Director Leon Panetta didn't hesitate to enthusiastically praise the drone attacks in Pakistan as "the only game in town." And best of all, they are "legal." We know this because the White House had the Justice Department prepare a 50-page document on their legality that it has refused to release to the public. In these campaigns in the backlands of distant places where there are seldom reporters, we nonetheless know that thousands of people have died, including significant numbers of children. Being run by a civilian agency, they cannot in any normal sense be "acts of war." In another world, they would certainly be considered illegal and possibly war crimes, as Christof Heyns, the U.N. special rapporteur on extrajudicial killings, has suggested. Top officials have taken responsibility for these acts, including the drone killings in Yemen of four American citizens condemned to death by a White House that has enthusiastically taken on the role of judge, jury, and executioner. No one involved, however, will ever see a day in court.

Perjury Before Congress

Lying to Congress in public testimony is, of course, perjury. Among others, we know that Director of National Intelligence James Clapper committed it in a strikingly bald-faced way on March 12, 2013. When asked by Senator Ron Wyden whether the NSA had gathered "any type of data at all on millions or hundreds of millions of Americans"—a question submitted to him a day in advance—Clapper answered, "No, sir. Not wittingly. There are cases where they could inadvertently perhaps collect, but not wittingly." This was a lie, pure and simple, as the Snowden revelations on the

NSA's gathering of phone metadata on all Americans (including, assumedly, our congressional representatives) would later make clear. Clapper subsequently apologized, saying that he spoke in what he called "the least untruthful" way possible, which, were crime on anyone's mind, would essentially have been a confession. Congress did nothing. Just in case you wondered, Clapper remains the director of national intelligence with the "support" of the president.

Mind you, the above seven categories don't even take into account the sort of warrantless surveillance of Americans that should have put someone in a court of law, or the ways in which various warrior corporations overbilled or cheated the government in its war zones, or the ways private contractors "ran wild" in those same zones. Even relatively low-level crimes by minor figures in the national security state have normally not been criminalized. Take, for example, the private surveillance of and cyberstalking of "love interests," or "LOVEINT," by NSA employees using government surveillance systems. The NSA claims that at least one employee was "disciplined" for this, but no one was taken to court. A rare exception: a number of low-level military figures in the Abu Ghraib scandal were tried for their abusive actions, convicted, and sent to jail, though no one higher than a colonel was held accountable in court for those infamously systematic and organized acts of torture and abuse.

Too Big to Fail, National Security–Style

All in all, as with the banks after the meltdown of 2007–2008, even the most obvious of national security state crimes seem to fall into a "too big to fail"-like category. Call it "too big to jail." The only crime that repeatedly makes it out of the investigative phase and into court—as with Stephen Kim, Chelsea Manning, and John Kiriakou—is revealing information the national security state holds dear. On that, the Obama administration has been fierce and prosecutorial.

Despite the claims of national security breaches in such cases, most of the leakers and whistleblowers of our moment have had little to offer in the way of information that might benefit Washington's official enemies. What Kim told Fox News about the North Korean nuclear program was hardly likely to have been news to the North Koreans, just as the Iranians are believed to have already known what General Cartwright may have leaked to the *Times* about the origins of the Stuxnet virus.

Of course, leaking is a habit that's often considered quite useful by those in power. It's little short of a sport in Washington, done whenever officials feel it to be to their advantage or the advantage of an administration, even if what's at stake are "secret" programs like the CIA's drone campaign in Pakistan. What's still up in the air—and to be tested—is whether leaking information in the government's supposed interest could, in fact, be a crime. And that's where General Cartwright comes in. If there is, in fact, but a single crime that can be committed within the national security state for which our leaders now believe jail time is appropriate, how wide is the category and is knowledge always a crime when it ends up in the wrong brains?

If there were one man of power and prominence who might join Kim, Kiriakou, Manning, and Edward Snowden (should the US government ever get its hands on him), it might be Cartwright. It's a long shot, but here's what he doesn't have going for him. He was an insider who was evidently an outsider. He was considered "a lone wolf" who went to the president privately, behind the backs of, and to the evident dismay of, the chairman of the Joint Chiefs and the Secretary of Defense. He seems to have had few supporters in the Pentagon and to have alienated key Republican senators. He could, in short, prove the single sacrificial lamb in the national security state.

In Washington today, knowledge is the only crime. That's a political reality of the twenty-first century. Get used to it.

9

Whistleblowers and Leakers Are Necessary to Keep the Government Transparent

Vanessa Baird

Vanessa Baird joined the New Internationalist *as a co-editor in 1986 and since then has written on everything from migration, money, religion, and equality to indigenous activism, climate change, feminism, and global LGBTQ rights. She also edits the mixed media, arts, and culture section of the magazine. She is the author of several books, including* The No-Nonsense Guide to World Population; Sex, Love and Homophobia; *and* People First Economics. *She is the recipient of the 2012 Amnesty International Human Rights Media award.*

Historically, whistleblowers and leakers who expose government secrets have been supported by the public but severely punished by the government. Vanessa Baird argues that it is necessary to have more legal protections for whistleblowers. The government claims whistleblowers are a threat to national security, but they do not provide evidence of the threats supposedly caused by leaks. Baird asserts that whistleblowing should be encouraged in order to protect the public interests. Because of the threats of government retaliation outlined in this viewpoint, journalists now recommend that whistleblowers act anonymously.

I s this the age of the whistleblower?
It would seem so, from the column inches, air time and cyberspace given to Edward Snowden.

According to campaigners, the 29-year-old former systems analyst at the US National Security Agency (NSA) is close to being the perfect whistleblower.

A quick look at the video clip interview with Laura Poitras shows why.[1] Measured, thoughtful, Snowden comes across as your average guy, intelligent but with no political axe to grind. He just thinks we should know that the secret services are capturing and storing every phone call we make or internet message we send and that our privacy is being violated wholesale. And he thinks we should at least debate whether we are happy with that or not.

His modest demeanour, his very ordinariness, is in sharp contrast to the scale and impact of his revelations. The sheer amount of data he was able to pass on to select media—some 1.7 million files—beats Chelsea Manning's impressive 251,287 diplomatic cables into a hat.

Since the advent of Wikileaks, whistleblowing has gone from being a "cottage" to an "industrialized" activity, to use the analogy suggested by Icelandic information activist Smári McCarthy.

Yet for most who do it, making disclosures about wrongdoing is a lonely, limiting and isolating affair. It's not like being on a production line with your mates.

Paradoxically, this also applies to the most celebrated. Edward Snowden and Wikileaks founder Julian Assange may have achieved rock-star status but they are fugitives, effectively exiled. Chelsea (formerly Bradley) Manning is serving 35 years in a military jail.

The Obama administration, for all its rhetoric of free speech, has started more prosecutions against whistleblowers than all presidents combined since 1917.[2]

"War against whistleblowers is a toxic trend," says Jesslyn Radack, Snowden's lawyer and a former US Justice Department whistleblower herself.[3]

And not just in the US. Japan recently approved sweeping government powers to punish those who would expose awkward truths about the country's nuclear industry, following the Fukushima disaster.[4]

A Dangerous Vocation

At the source of most exposures of wrongdoing is not a government regulator or police investigator or even an investigative journalist, but a whistleblower. A moral insider who breaks ranks to tell the truth about the malpractice she or he sees.

Once the scandal has broken, such people will be hailed as heroes, admired for their integrity by a public grateful that such courageous and outspoken people exist.

But gratitude offers no protection.

In 2010, millions of Chinese parents were horrified to find that their children were drinking milk that had become mixed with toxic chemicals at fresh milk collection points. Two years later, one of the two men who exposed the practice, farmer Jiang Weisuo, was murdered in circumstances that have never been explained.

More recent is the case of Lawrence Moepi, a fearless and principled South African auditor, dubbed the "fraudsters' worst nightmare." Last October, as he arrived at his Johannesburg office, he was shot and killed by, it is believed, hired assassins. He had been investigating several suspected corruption cases, including a notorious arms deal.

Silencing or exacting retribution can take many forms, violent and direct—or more devious.

Craig Murray, a former British ambassador who exposed how the British and US secret services were supporting torture in Uzbekistan, was subsequently accused of asking for sex in exchange for visas. It took him 18 months to clear his name.

Janice Karpinsky, the most senior woman in the US army, was arrested and accused of shoplifting the day after revealing that Donald Rumsfeld ordered the torture of prisoners at Abu Ghraib.

Murray comments: "Whistleblowers are rare because it is a near suicidal vocation and everyone else is too scared to help. And if your whistleblowing involves the world of war and spying, they will try to set you up on false charges... and not just sack you but destroy you."[5]

While public opinion is generally on the side of whistleblowers, governments, institutions and employers are not. When it comes to the really embarrassing and damaging disclosures, those in power will do all they can to turn the revealer into the enemy.

This has worked on a significant minority of the US public, furious with Manning and Snowden for allegedly putting at risk the security of all Americans. When pressed to say exactly how, the political and secret service players have failed to come up with one concrete example, resorting to vague comments about "agents in the field" and the fact that "terrorists will now change their tactics." These are high-profile, international cases. But most whistleblowing happens at a far more modest, local level. Sometimes the revelations will reach the local press or emerge during an employment tribunal after the discloser has been dismissed or demoted. Often media outlets are afraid to investigate the information whistleblowers bring them, because they cannot take the risk of a costly libel or defamation suit, or because the story is too complicated or time-consuming to corroborate.

Legal Protection

"Effective whistleblowing arrangements are a key part of good governance," says the British organization Public Concern At Work (PCaW). "A healthy and open culture is one where people are encouraged to speak out, confident that they can do so without adverse repercussions, confident that they will be listened to, and confident that appropriate action will be taken."

If only. In the topsy-turvy world of whistleblowing it tends to be the person revealing wrongdoing, rather than the wrongdoer, who is punished and who ends up losing most—typically their job and career, but often also their relationship, their home, even their liberty.

The complex dynamics at play when someone discloses unwelcome information are explored by psychoanalyst David

Morgan in his article "I had to do it." Far from being rebels and outsiders, most disclosers are diligent, conscientious, somewhat obsessive insiders, who think their employers will be grateful for the information given and will naturally want to do the right thing.

An increasing number of countries have laws on their statute books—with more in the pipeline—specifically to protect whistleblowers from retaliation, harassment or victimization. But most laws are severely limited in their scope and effectiveness. For example, in Canada and Australia, the law does not apply to people working in the private sector, while New Zealand's law is limited to government agencies.[6,7]

In Canada, a fierce libel regime contributes to creating possibly the most hostile environment in the English-speaking world. Britain is one of the few European countries with a law that applies across both private and public sectors, but in practice British whistleblowers do not fare too well either and libel laws that favour the rich have a chilling effect.[8] US law is patchy and contradictory, extremely hostile to those who speak out in some areas, but enabling large financial rewards for those who disclose fraud against the government.[9]

While whistleblowers may need to be compensated for loss of earnings, the awarding of massive cash settlements is controversial. Cathy James of the British PCaW sees "moral hazard" in a US-style system. In her view: "Whistleblowing should be seen as a very positive issue, everyone should be encouraged to protect the public interest. I don't want to live in a society where people do the right things because they think they are going to benefit."

Going public on confidential information may put disclosers on the wrong side of the law, especially if they have smuggled out documents or broken official secrecy arrangements. This has led to absurd examples, like that of the banker Bradley Birkenfeld who exposed $780 million tax fraud at UBS, receiving a Swiss prison sentence for breaking confidentiality.

Under British law, disclosers who break the law to reveal wrongdoing can claim, in their defence, that they were acting in the "public interest." This is not widely available elsewhere (see the case of Chelsea Manning in "Dead bastards").

"I Now Recommend Leaking"

Considerable energy goes into lobbying for laws and practices to protect properly those who speak out and many whistleblower organizations believe this is the way forward.[10]

Brian Martin is a veteran campaigner with Whistleblowers Australia who has talked with hundreds of disclosers and written a highly regarded practical guide on the topic.

And he has come to the conclusion that the intense focus on legal protection is misguided.

"It seldom works and can even make whistleblowers more vulnerable; they think they are protected but aren't."

Instead, he now encourages potential disclosers to develop their skills and understanding so that they can be more effective in bringing about change. The most effective strategies, he says, involve taking messages to a wider audience, through mass media, social media or direct communication.

"I now recommend leaking—anonymous whistleblowing—whenever possible."

This may not come naturally to most disclosers, who are conscientious employees who believe the system works. They will try official channels first and are reluctant to contact the media or action groups.

But, Martin points out, whistleblowers are "hardly ever effective in challenging the problems they attempt to expose. This sounds pessimistic. Whistleblowers are courageous but they need a lot of help to be more effective. Probably the best scenario is a link-up between a network of leakers and well-connected action groups."

Smári McCarthy is another activist who is moving away from the legal protection route. For three years he, and others in his native Iceland, worked to create a model legal environment for leakers, whistleblowers and journalists. They were making good headway until April 2013 when a rightwing coalition government came to power and stalled reform.

Now he is focusing more on technology. There are two laws, he says, that governments have to obey: "physics and economics." He plans to use the former to make mass surveillance—whereby intelligence services gather everybody's private internet and phone communication—too expensive to do.

He has calculated that the total budget of the "Five Eyes"— that is the communications snooping services of the US, Britain, Australia, Canada and New Zealand combined—is $120 billion a year. With that they can scoop up the data of 2.5 billion internet users, making the cost per person per day a mere 13 cents.

"My five-year plan is to increase that cost to $10,000 per person per day. The services would have to be a lot more selective and do their job properly."

How to do it? Encryption—the types that hackers have developed and which the NSA has still, as far as we know, not managed to crack. "I use encryption a lot," says McCarthy. "But we need to make it easier to use and available to everyone."

This will help disclosers too, he says, because if everybody's privacy is improved then so is that of whistleblowers. Naturally, their leaks need to be accurate, need to pass the "public interest" test and not gratuitously violate personal privacy.

Snowden and others have revealed the extent to which free speech and civil liberties are being violated by the state, and not just in countries like Russia or China.

More and more information is being classified as top secret and we have no way of debating whether or not it should be.[11] The recent Stasi-style destruction of laptops at the *Guardian* newspaper, under the supervision of Britain's GCHQ, should serve as a warning. As they say, democracy dies behind closed doors—and now too in smashed hard-drives in newspaper offices.

Those genuinely engaged in disclosing in the public interest need protection all along the communication line—from sources and whistleblowers, through campaigners and journalists, to print or web publishers and distributors. In 2011, under a social-democrat government, Iceland followed Council of Europe recommendations and made it illegal for journalists to expose their sources. In Britain a journalist can be jailed for not doing so. It is even worse in the US: Barrett Brown, a young freelancer, is facing 105 years in prison in connection with the posting of information that hackers obtained from Statfor, a private intelligence company with close ties to the federal government.[12]

A Better World

At its heart, whistleblowing is about the desire for truth to be known, for things to be done properly, and for the world to be made a better place.

A place where big business does not cheat or harm citizens for profit; where hospitals and care homes look after frail and elderly people and banks do not rob their customers. Where politicians see office as public service rather than self-service, priests respect the bodily integrity of children in their charge and military personnel do not go on shooting sprees for the hell of it.

Sometimes exposure yields tangible results and the information revealed improves or even saves lives. In 1994, US paralegal Merrell Williams leaked internal memos from Brown & Williamson Tobacco company that showed that the company knew it was lying when it claimed that cigarettes were not harmful, that nicotine was not addictive and that it did not market to children.

His action fuelled lawsuits that resulted in an industry pay-out of billions of dollars to pay smokers' medical bills.[13]

Whistleblowers act as the guardians of morality, but too often they are solitary martyrs to democracy. As Wikileaks revealed towards the end of last year, the world is currently facing a major multilateral threat to democracy. It is coming not from religious fanatics in turbans but from fundamentalists in suits.

The acronyms TPP and TTIP are enough to lead even the most committed insomniac to the land of nod. But stay awake, please!

This is important. These are US-led international trade deals being negotiated—in conditions of unprecedented secrecy—that will give corporations the power to trump national sovereignty and the interests of billions of people. Two secret drafts of the TransPacific Partnership (TPP), obtained by Wikileaks, on intellectual property and the environment show the deals would trample over individual rights and free expression and give powerful companies the right to challenge domestic laws regulating, for example, resource extraction in Peru or Australia. The Transatlantic Trade and Investment Partnership (TTIP)—between the US and the EU— would have a similar impact, making existing national public services such as health and education even more vulnerable to aggressive action by big private corporations from outside. Those trying to save Britain's national health service from the clutches of private US medical companies know how bad this could be.

Such trade agreements are made at a high level, hatched between a nexus of powerful corporations, governments that do their bidding and secret services that we now know (again, thanks to Snowden) really do use public money to spy on behalf of big business.

The only thing that will counteract the undemocratic and self-serving power of this nexus is a growing network from below that involves whistleblowers, civil society activists and hactivists, journalists and citizens who care.[14]

Only if we have access to information do we have democracy—and today the most relevant information often comes from whistleblowers.

Only if we can participate, is that democracy real—which is why we need to use the information to take action and stop sleepwalking into totalitarianism, be it that of a corrupt institution or a world order devised by and for a global, corporate élite.

Then the tremendous risks that whistleblowers take, and the sacrifices they make, will not be in vain.

References

1. https://www.theguardian.com/world/video/2013/jun/09/nsa-whistleblower-edward-snowden-interview-vi

2. http://www.abc.net.au/news/2013-08-16/assange-obama-whistleblower/4856762

3. 29C3 panel

4. The *Ecologist*

5. Craig Murray craigmurray.org.uk

6. Canada's Public Servants Disclosure Act 2000; Australia's Public Interest Disclosure Act 2013

7. Protected Disclosure Act 2000

8. Public Interest Disclosure Act 1998

9. False Claims Act; Dodd-Frank Wall Street Reforms

10. The Whistleblowing Commission is calling for a mandatory code of practice

11. Paste Bin

12. Government Accountability Project

13. *New York Times*

14. For example, the Alternative Trade Mandate Network.

10

The Success of Social Movements Proves the Deep State Does Not Exist

Anthony DiMaggio

Anthony DiMaggio received his PhD in political communication from the University of Illinois at Chicago. He is the author of several books, including The Rise of the Tea Party: Political Discontent and Corporate Media in the Age of Obama.

Mike Lofgren was a member of Congress for close to thirty years. After retiring, he wrote a book titled The Deep State: The Fall of the Constitution and the Rise of a Shadow Government, *in which he explains the influence of corporations on the US government and how it makes the political process less democratic. Viewpoint author Anthony DiMaggio initially found Lofgren's description of civil servants compelling, but he ultimately determined there is no proof of a deep state at work in America. While the NSA does act as a kind of panopticon—a centralized system of surveillance—DiMaggio asserts there is no proof of a shadow government at work. He argues that the ability of social movements to change society and laws proves there is no deep state controlling the government.*

The stratospheric rise of Mike Lofgren's "deep state" critique has been matched only by its meteoric fall into the pits of conspiracy theory and caricature. What started off as a potentially interesting analytical framework, which sought to spotlight the

"Ditching the 'Deep State': The Rise of a New Conspiracy Theory in American Politics," by Anthony DiMaggio, CounterPunch, March 24, 2017. Reprinted by permission.

US corporate-national security-intelligence apparatus, has quickly devolved into a cartoonish absurdity. This decline was predictable considering that the "deep state" analysis provided by Lofgren was such an expansive, vague concept from the start. The "deep state" framework lacked the nuance of previous versions of "elite theory" developed over the decades, so its adoption by various rightwing partisan stooges and conspiracy theorists doesn't surprise me. We have now reached the point where the "deep state" rhetoric is no longer useful, and has even become harmful to informed political discourse on American politics.

I will say from the outset that I admire Mike Lofgren, a former Congressman, for drawing attention to the rise of corporate power and the ever-expanding, runaway military state. His book, *The Deep State: The Fall of the Constitution and the Rise of a Shadow Government*, appears to be a genuine, heartfelt effort to fight back against the reactionary forces that control American politics. And his main concerns with the American political system are warranted. He is right to focus on the dangers of the growing national security state, coordinated largely through the NSA and other agencies, and to condemn their assault on citizens' privacy rights. Lofgren adopts the metaphor of the panopticon to describe the security state, referring to Jeremy Bentham's conceptual prison design, which was comprised of a circular structure with a central "watchman" tower. The structure is designed so that prisoners cannot tell whether a guard can see them at any given time, despite the central location of the tower, which suggests that the state could be watching you at any moment.

The use of the panopticon as a symbol of the modern-day surveillance state is apt. The NSA, while not recording every phone call in the United States, keeps records of these calls, allowing for closer inspections of conversations on a case-by-case basis. Even if the state is not technically recording every word we speak, it always has its eye on the American people, and is ready to intervene at a moment's notice. Drawing on the panopticon, Lofgren refers to the rise of "militarized authoritarianism" via the growing power of the US intelligence apparatus, and I find it hard to disagree with him.

Lofgren is also right to emphasize other threats to American democracy. He laments the rise of corporate profiteering in the "War on Terror," calling back to warnings from decades' past about the US military industrial complex. Corporate and political actors profit from hundreds of billions a year spent on a bloated "national security" state, at the expense of social spending on education, health care, and infrastructural needs. In an era of record inequality, the fixation of US political and economic elites on militarism exacts a huge cost, draining much needed financial resources that could be allocated toward rebuilding the country and providing for the basic needs of the citizenry.

Finally, Lofgren's concern with the rise of Wall Street power, which has coincided with the financialization of the US economy, is timely and welcome. Financial deregulation is one of the greatest threats to our economy, and the failure of both political parties to limit the power of financial elites is one of the great tragedies of modern times. The American banking system has historically been a parasitic force in the American economy. Wall Street's speculation on vital goods such as oil, housing, internet stocks, and other goods has fed stock market bubbles, the collapse of which wreak havoc on the economy and American workers, draining their retirement savings, and fueling the rise of unemployment and underemployment. Financialization undermines the economy— which is now largely driven by speculators and characterized by anemic to non-existent economic growth. What profit gains exist are now largely captured by financial and other corporate elites. Meanwhile, the masses of Americans find themselves working longer hours, with increased productivity, for stagnating to declining wages, amidst huge increases in cost-of-living via out-of-control health care and education costs.

Despite the serious and legitimate concerns that Lofgren raises, there are several serious problems with the "deep state" framework. These problems become harder to deny as Lofgren's work gains prominence among American pundits, intellectuals, and political elites. Lofgren popularized the "deep state" term, referring to "a hybrid of national security and law enforcement agencies, plus key parts of other branches whose roles given them membership. The Department of Defense, the Department of State, the Department of Homeland Security, the Central Intelligence Agency, and the Justice Department are all part of the Deep State." But the "deep state" concept lacked nuance and clarity, making it ripe for adoption by partisan hacks and conspiracy theorists. This is not to attack Lofgren for promoting a conspiracy theory, as he is clear in his book that he is providing an institutional analysis of the threats to American democracy. In fact, I find claims that Lofgren is a conspiracy theorist to be rather bizarre and ill-informed. If anything, his analysis comes off as somewhat tame within the broader intellectual history of elite theory, in that he fails to identify corporate capitalism as the primary threat to the US economy and to the American public. Lofgren is no socialist or Marxist, and his analysis is somewhat pedestrian and conservative in that he eschews traditional efforts at institutional analysis that incorporate Marxian tools for spotlighting systemic repression such as alienated labor, economic determinism, hegemony, and commodity fetishism.

Because of the vague nature of the "deep state," it has become a Rorschach test for American pundits and citizens alike. It is something upon which they can impute whatever beliefs or values they have. It can mean whatever one wants it to mean. Reactionary partisan hacks like Sean Hannity, Newt Gingrich, Andrew Napolitano, and Sean Spicer freely adopt the term to refer to allegedly pro-Obama elements within the US government and intelligence apparatus. Hannity takes aim at "the liberal media" and "American intelligence agencies," the latter of which he claims is dominated by a "deep state swamp of Obama holdover DC lifers" who are "hell-bent on destroying Trump." Of course, Hannity has raised no concern with an emerging deep state swamp of Trump DC lifers populated by plutocratic billionaires, as the president moves to populate the federal bureaucracy with his preferred political supporters and hacks.

We have also seen the rise of conspiratorial rhetoric on "the left" regarding the ominous "deep state." I'll refrain from identifying any specific person by name (fratricide is not an endearing trait), but the depth of conspiracy-mongering "deep state" absurdity has clearly afflicted various leftist critics of the American political system. Over the last year, various leftists framed the "deep state" as a secret shadow government, impervious to any controls or regulation by elected officials. It is said to represent a miniature government within the larger government, and it is so nefariously effective that it ensures the American people have zero political influence over American politics. Forget about social movements or protests. They're pointless. The secret paper-pushers of the "deep state" have already ensured that representation of the masses is a fiction. Don't even bother with protest or social action—there's really nothing you can do to promote progressive political change. Furthermore, forget about efforts to stifle US militarism abroad. The "deep state" shadow government secretly pulls the strings of political officials such as Barack Obama, forcing him to escalate wars in Afghanistan and elsewhere, despite growing anti-war sentiment at home.

It should be clear from anyone who studies American history how absurd these claims are. While those on the left have long known that the US political system is captured by corporate power and wealth, to suggest that social movement activism and opposition to the status quo are bound to fail is a horrifically misinformed position, and is contradicted by history itself. The last century of US political activism demonstrates that large numbers of social movements were able to fundamentally transform American culture and politics, as seen in the women's rights movement, the struggle for civil rights, the rise of modern environmentalism and the struggle against nuclear power, the successes of organized labor activism, the gay and lesbian rights movement, and numerous other progressive uprisings.

Furthermore, to claim that appointed "deep state" bureaucrats hold all the power in Washington, at the expense of elected officials, is equally outlandish. Lofgren doesn't even try to make this claim in his book, as he refers to "deep state" operatives in the US bureaucracy as largely "order-takers," serving those who visibly hold power as elected officials or as heads of "national security-related" federal agencies.

Lofgren is right not to frame elected officials as slaves to faceless bureaucrats, and one can see the silliness of such depictions when looking at recent history. For example, looking at the case of the 2009 escalation of the war in Afghanistan, the troop "surge" (which occurred in phases throughout the year) was explicitly supported by Obama when he ran in the 2008 election. Furthermore, anyone closely paying attention to the news at the time could have recognized that the fight between Obama and General Stanley McChrystal (and other elements of US military leadership) was not over whether to expand the war in Afghanistan, but over how quickly to escalate and drawdown the war, and over how many forces would be committed. In other words, the "fight" was over strategy and logistics, not principle or substance. It should be pointed out, by the way, that Obama won this logistical battle with the generals, announcing a smaller infusion of troops than McChrystal wanted, attached to a date (of 2011) in which a drawdown was supposed to begin. This deadline was opposed by the generals (for the story on the surge, see: Peter Baker, "How Obama Came to Plan for 'Surge' in Afghanistan," *New York Times,* December 5, 2009).

I don't mean to marginalize concerns that the US is witnessing a creeping authoritarianism, via the growing strength of our institutionalized military-intelligence state. I agree that this is occurring, and is a serious threat to the country. But depictions of US elected leaders as puppets of the bureaucracy—the latter of which retain all the power in US politics—are outlandish caricatures of how the political system really works. Furthermore, we insult the victims of the fully-fledged dictatorships of the world by depicting

Americans as suffering under some sort of comparable military dictatorship (remember the "deep state" terminology was originally developed in reference to Turkey). There is simply no equivalent in the United States to the mass torture and mass killings engaged in by brutal dictatorships of history run by Mubarak in Egypt, Assad in Syria, or Erdogan in Turkey, among others. Certainly the US has its own unique and repressive version of a militarized police system, which has long been used to criminalize and suppress minorities and protesters. But to ignore the obvious differences between the US and dictatorships regarding the presence of basic political freedoms to say what one wishes, and to openly disagree with government, is to engage in a distortion of epic proportions.

As an aside, it is also worth pointing out that the US intelligence community is nowhere near as uniform as "deep state" conspiracies claim. Members of the US "security" state have at times sought to pressure elected officials, with harmful effects on democracy. A few recent examples include the hysteria voiced by agencies like the CIA over Russia's alleged interference in the US election, and in which Democrats have claimed, without presenting evidence, that Vladimir Putin effectively threw the election in favor of Trump. Another example of wheeling and dealing by the intelligence community is the Afghanistan surge. It seems clear, despite Obama's pro-surge inclinations, that the attacks from McChrystal and the US military did create additional pressure on the Obama administration to escalate war.

Recognizing that the US intelligence community and military apparatus have power in the political process, however, does not mean that these officials always serve state power or imperial interests. One can look no further than the 2007 National Intelligence Estimate, which represented a collective middle finger to the Bush administration from the intelligence community, on the issue of whether Iran was developing nuclear weapons. Members of the intelligence community were clearly angry at the egg left on their faces following the embarrassment that was the 2002 NIE, which sugar-coated the Bush administration's case for war with Iraq. Subsequent historical accounts documented how the intelligence community, particularly analysts at the CIA, were bullied by high-level members of the Bush administration in the pre-war period to "get behind" the president and the war effort. The 2007 NIE represented a comprehensive effort on the part of the intelligence community to pump the breaks on Bush's imperial war agenda, and it was effective in defusing the case for war. The push against war with Iran was not an isolated incident, either. It should be clear by taking a longer historical view recognizing the many intelligence analysts willing to question US militarism and imperialism by leaking sensitive and classified information to the press. Whether one is talking about "Deep Throat" (Mark Felt) or Daniel Ellsberg in the Nixon era, or anonymous intelligence analysts feeding critical information to news outlets like Knight Ridder prior to the 2003 Iraq war, or more recent whistleblowers like Chelsea Manning and Edward Snowden, the US intelligence community is not all of one mind about US militarism and empire.

[...]

To put it simply, elite theory has come a long way over the last half-century, and especially since the 2008 economic crash. Because of the explosion in the last decade of studies of elite power, we know more about the American plutocracy than ever before. Considering this new informational environment, Lofgren's book provides an interesting reflection on the experiences of one man in Congress over the decades, and it is a welcome addition to the discussion of elitism in government. But it is not clear how much his "deep state" framework tells us about US policy than we already knew.

[...]

11

The Bureaucrats That Some Call "the Deep State" Are Essential to Democracy

David Spence

David Spence is a professor of law, politics, and regulation at the McCombs School of Business and the University of Texas School of Law. He regularly contributes to legal journals and has been published by the Huffington Post, Fortune, *and the* Washington Post.

David Spence argues that calling unelected bureaucrats who check executive power "the deep state" results in an undeserved negative connotation. Spence argues that it is the responsibility of unelected bureaucrats to not simply serve the president but to uphold the law, and that sometimes ensuring that the rule of law is maintained involves going against the wishes of the president. He asserts that there is a longstanding tradition of bureaucrats defending their agency's mission despite changes in executive leadership, with the judicial system assisting in these efforts. What some consider the deep state is in fact a normal part of a healthy democracy.

Some of the recent news coverage of executive-branch resistance to the Trump agenda has invoked the notion of the "deep state," a phrase hinting at sinister, unelected bureaucrats undermining the agenda of an elected president. But bureaucratic resistance to presidential control does not necessarily subvert democracy. To the contrary, it often affirms it.

"Founders Might Have Liked 'Deep State,'" by David Spence, The University of Texas at Austin, March 20, 2017. http://www.texasenterprise.utexas.edu/2017/03/20/deep-state /Trump-deep-state-government-agencies. Licensed under CC BY-SA 3.0.

Executive-branch careerists—bureaucrats—have long been the whipping boys of our political discourse. Whenever voters, commentators or politicians don't like agency policies, it is easy to blame "unelected bureaucrats" acting in anti-democratic ways.

But remember, Congress and the president use statutes to define the missions of executive-branch agencies, and agency staff consists mostly of people who are committed to that mission. The people who work at the Securities and Exchange Commission are dedicated to policing capital markets to ensure that they are fair. The people who work at the Food and Drug Administration are dedicated to protecting consumers from harmful drugs. And the people who work at the Environmental Protection Agency are dedicated to environmental protection.

Sometimes presidents appoint agency heads who try to subvert that statutory mission from within. This is nothing new. Anne Gorsuch Burford, mother of current Supreme Court nominee Neil Gorsuch, was forced to resign her position as Ronald Reagan's first EPA administrator partly because agency careerists effectively mustered public and congressional opposition to her leadership. This dynamic is sufficiently common that academics have studied it for decades.

The crucial point is this: In our democracy, public preferences get translated into policy through lawmaking, not simply through elections. The election of any president does not necessarily signify a public desire to change an agency's mission or repeal any particular law.

Meanwhile, executive-branch agencies remain obliged to implement the securities laws, food and drug laws, environmental laws, and the various other statutes that define the modern administrative state. This is part of what we mean by "the rule of law," and it is entirely consistent with the Framers' desire for government to produce policy decisions that resist the kind of temporary passions that loom so large in today's polarized politics, and instead reflect the "permanent and aggregate interests of the community," as James Madison framed it in Federalist No. 10.

To be sure, it is the president's constitutional role to oversee agencies as they discharge their statutory duties. But that process must always remain within statutory boundaries. If a president is unhappy with the basic mission of the SEC, FDA, or EPA, the appropriate remedy is to redefine that mission through legislation. When the president instead tries to undermine that mission by appointing an agency head willing to try to subvert it, resistance by careerists doesn't undermine democracy or the rule of law—rather, it vindicates those principles.

Certainly, overzealous agencies sometimes stretch their statutory authority beyond recognition. In those instances we rely on the courts to keep agencies in their jurisdictional lanes and to enforce the rule of law. Hence all the litigation reviewing the Obama administration's implementation of the Affordable Care Act, the Clean Air Act, and other laws.

But courts will also discipline presidents who try to steer an agency away from its statutory mission. That is how President George W. Bush's EPA lost a succession of high-profile court cases challenging its interpretations of the Clean Air Act. The Trump administration's recent promise not to replace the Clean Power Plan may meet the same fate.

The Trump administration has made clear its intent to roll back regulation in ways that may contradict agencies' enabling legislation. When that happens, expect courts to push back. If Republicans want to "deconstruct" the administrative state, as Trump senior adviser Stephen K. Bannon says, changing presidents is not enough. They will have to change the law.

12

Referring to Civil Servants as "the Deep State" Fosters Distrust

Charles S. Clark

Charles S. Clark joined Government Executive *in the fall of 2009. He has been on staff at the* Washington Post, Congressional Quarterly, National Journal, *Time-Life Books, Tax Analysts, the Association of Governing Boards of Universities and Colleges, and the National Center on Education and the Economy. He has written and edited online news, daily news stories, long-form features, wire copy, magazines, books, and organizational media strategies.*

Despite President Trump's claims, Charles S. Clark argues that the deep state is an inaccurate description of how government works. Characterizing civil servants as members of the deep state delegitimizes their roles in the eyes of the government. In reality, long-term civil servants are needed for the government to function properly. When the government downsizes civil servants, not only do people lose their jobs, but the institutional knowledge of each civil servant is lost as well. Clark claims that when members of the government start accusing each other of being involved in a shadow government, it fosters distrust, and a divided government gets little done.

"Deconstructing the Deep State," by Charles S. Clark, Government Executive Media Group, August 15, 2017. Reprinted by permission.

A month after President Trump took the oath of office, his chief strategist offered a controversial description of what Americans, including the 2 million career civil servants Trump now leads in the executive branch, could expect from the new president: Every day would be a battle for "deconstruction of the administrative state," said Stephen Bannon, the man frequently described as the mastermind behind Trump's nationalist agenda.

Bannon is no longer in the White House, but his remarks at a conservative political conference in February continue to reverberate through government.

Some interpreted Bannon's comment as a reference to Trump's classic Republican goals of reducing regulations, cutting taxes and shrinking government. But in a Manichean speech in Warsaw, Poland, in July, Trump warned of a danger "invisible to some but familiar to the Poles: the steady creep of government bureaucracy that drains the vitality and wealth of the people."

As the Trump era has unfolded, the term "deep state" has come to mean something sinister to some on the far right. More than just signifying an impersonal, inept bureaucracy, it conjures a secretive illuminati of bureaucrats determined to sabotage the Trump agenda.

On the pro-Trump Mark Levin radio show, commentator Dan Bongino decried the ongoing investigation of Trump's ties to the Russians during the 2016 campaign, saying, "They want a scalp, and believe me when I tell you the deep state is going to get one."

Trump is being attacked, said a memo from a National Security Council staffer published in August by *Foreign Policy*, because he represents "an existential threat to cultural Marxist memes that dominate the prevailing cultural narrative." Those threatened by Trump include "deep state actors, globalists, bankers, Islamists, and establishment Republicans."

In July, Breitbart News—where Bannon presided before joining the Trump presidential campaign in August 2016, and to which he immediately returned after his departure from the White House a year later—publicized a report from the Senate Homeland Security and Governmental Affairs Committee saying Trump faced seven times more leaks during the first 126 days of his administration than the previous two administrations.

"How many foreign allies are pulling back?" asked the *Wall Street Journal's* Kimberley Strassel in a column titled "Washington's Leak Mob." "How many will work with a US government that has disclosed so many military plans, weapons systems and cybersecurity tactics?"

A Hostile Takeover

Even before he took the oath of office, Trump took to Twitter to characterize suspected leakers in the intelligence community as behaving like Nazis. At the Justice Department, Attorney General Jeff Sessions in August issued a loud warning to would-be leakers, even as some career Justice staff continued spilling to the media their worries about Sessions' policy reversals on such issues as immigration and affirmative action.

Also enlisting in the war against the deep state are right-leaning legal activists who use the Freedom of Information Act to target disgruntled career federal workers who use encrypted software to make anonymous political commentary unflattering to Trump.

But to many with years in government, the term "deep state" is disturbing. "Deep state is both inaccurate and grossly misleading," said Nancy McEldowney, who retired in June as director of the Arlington, Va.-based Foreign Service Institute. "The term originated in the context of analyzing the situations in Turkey and Egypt, where I served, usually to talk about propaganda, dirty tricks, and even violence to overthrow the government," she said.

"To refer to career civil servants in the US government as some form of deep state is a clear attempt to delegitimize voices of disagreement," she added. "Even worse, it carries with it the potential for fear-baiting and rumor-mongering, and is really a dark conspiratorial term that does not correspond to reality."

Chris Lu, President Obama's deputy Labor secretary, rejects the notion that some entrenched deep state is undermining Trump's political appointees. "The politicals set the direction of the agency, but they can only do it effectively if they tap into the expertise of the federal civil service," he said.

Lu, now a senior fellow at the University of Virginia Miller Center of Public Affairs, says it's important to remember why the civil service was created under the 1883 Pendleton Act. "Before then, there were stories of the amounts of time [President] Lincoln spent meeting with job seekers, with ads in Washington newspapers selling jobs under the spoils system and the tradition of incoming administrations kicking everyone out," he said. Creation of the civil service was "one of the most important reforms of the past century and a half, and is one reason the federal government is still the most important and powerful organization in the world."

But if the Trump team is misreading how government works, it is not the first new administration to do so. Every new president brings into office political appointees who are wary of "bureaucrats," said Paul Light, Paulette Goddard Professor of Public Service at New York University. "Democrats historically have been as reluctant to work with careerists as Republicans, not because of the ideology but because of the desire for speed."

Democrats generally understand they will need federal employees to implement their policies, "though they may believe that those employees need to be liberated from rules," Light added. "Republicans have the same hierarchy, but are motivated by a different goal. Both parties in the past have come in saying, 'We've got an agenda; we've got four years, maybe eight, so we can't wait for action.'"

In the Trump administration, Light noted, many may agree with Bannon's concept of a deep state, but are uncomfortable with that language.

Others are skeptical that many in Trump's circles actually buy into the notion of a deep state. "If they had this theory of the deep state and were worried, the first thing they would do is appoint a lot of political appointees," said Donald Devine, who headed the Office of Personnel Management in the Reagan administration.

Norm Ornstein, a longtime observer of Washington at the American Enterprise Institute, is appalled at what he sees as Bannon's promotion of a "conspiracy theory of lawless people trying to undermine American values for their own warped sense and defying laws and property."

In fact, Ornstein said, "we have career people and some political appointees who've been there some time who are essential to the functioning of government. They've been there through many administrations and have their own policy interests." So yes, there is that web of people. "But my experience over many decades is that overwhelmingly they understand their role, and whether they like the policies or not, they follow the lead of administrations."

In recent decades, there's been "significant damage done," Ornstein added, "in that when there's a change in party, the newcomers tend to view many of those career people working for previous administrations as traitors you want to force out. The tensions are greater now in the era of polarized politics."

Distrust Cuts Both Ways

Trump's antipathy toward the career federal workforce may have been sealed on Inauguration Day, after a National Park Service employee retweeted Twitter messages comparing crowd sizes at the 2017 ceremony with those of the 2008 inauguration of President Obama. The effect, not favorable to Trump, prompted the new president to phone acting NPS Director Michael Reynolds to complain that his crowd size was underplayed. (A subsequent investigation by the Interior Department watchdog found no wrongdoing on the part of Park Service employees.)

One can see how this might have informed Trump's impression of a deep state. Just six weeks later, Trump accused President Obama of "wiretapping" his conversations at Trump Tower in New York.

More than half of federal employees had said the previous October they would vote for Hillary Clinton, according to a *Government Executive*/Government Business Council survey.

Just 34 percent were for Trump. (As many as a quarter of federal employees had said in an earlier *Government Executive*/GBC poll that they would resign were Trump to win the election.)

Campaign donations from federal employees for the 2016 cycle skewed toward Democrats, in some agencies by a factor of 10-to-1, according to the Center for Responsive Politics. In recent months, the news media, which Trump often derides as "fake," have published numerous essays and interviews with disgruntled federal employees, including one from a former State Department employee who accused Secretary Rex Tillerson of an "inherent distrust of the State Department and career officers."

And when Sessions in August announced a reversal of Justice's position on a case involving Ohio's effort to purge rolls of inactive voters, career staff who had signed a related brief during the Obama years did not put their names on the Trump version.

Many of Trump's staff and appointees had experience in previous Republican administrations, where, to varying degrees, political appointees came into agencies with an agenda to shrink the bureaucracy and make government less intrusive.

An Agenda With a Precedent

Indeed, President Reagan's "government is the problem" theme had its heyday only three years after Democratic President Jimmy Carter had worked with Congress to enact the 1978 Civil Service Act, largely as an effort to professionalize government.

Devine, who ran personnel-related issues for Reagan's transition team before becoming OPM director, recalls the scene in 1981 as one in which "unions were threatening job actions, and either sitting with their arms folded or not showing up." Eventually, after federal air traffic controllers went on strike and Reagan fired them, "those job actions stopped."

Most civil servants disliked Reagan. Devine, now a college professor, remembers an early speech on cutting bureaucracy he delivered to the American Society for Public Administration. It drew loud boos and multiple requests for printed copies. "My dealings with the bureaucracy showed me their first priorities were maintaining the status quo in their agencies, and they were certainly not Republicans," he said.

The Reagan years, much like today, brought to Washington many appointees to run agencies charged with missions the appointees don't endorse. One such example is Anne Gorsuch Burford, Reagan's Environmental Protection Agency administrator. In 1981, with Reagan's blessing, she began implementing a 22 percent budget cut and slashed regulations. After a scandal surrounding the $1.6 billion hazardous waste superfund cleanup program, she was cited for contempt of Congress. (Though Burford wouldn't have mentioned a deep state, she did say later that Washington was "too small to be a state but too large to be an asylum for the mentally deranged.")

Career employees working under Burford recall the pressure she was under to please Reagan campaign donors such as the Colorado-based Joseph Coors beer family, and how Budget Director David Stockman would target programs for elimination without any debate. "I received a call from my boss's deputy less than a month after the inauguration telling me my noise control program was being abolished, and the decision was not appealable," recalled Chuck Elkins, who spent 25 years at EPA. "We regulated an industry for their noise, and one of the manufacturers had complained to Stockman."

During the Reagan transition, Elkins attended a meeting where political appointees spoke frankly about favoring industry, he told *Government Executive*. He was deeply committed to the program's mission, and the message from the new administration was disturbing. "My first reaction was 'we can't lose this,'" Elkins said. But soon his thoughts turned to the 100 people who would lose their jobs at a time when he himself had two kids in college. He responded by setting up a clinic on resume writing. Soon most employees found jobs with the Navy or the Interior Department, where Elkins did a stint before eventually returning to EPA to work in other areas.

Burford feared the bureaucracy enough to compile "an enemies list," recalled Elkins' colleague Ed Hanley. He recalled being summoned by EPA's acting boss and handed "a yellow buck slip with seven names, all career," with instructions that he should "get on top of these people, or something vague and threatening like that," Hanley said.

It was left to Hanley to explain the limitations on firing career staff without cause. In the end, Burford signed off on some "questionable personnel actions to get her people in," Hanley recalls, but ultimately Burford herself was fired and Reagan brought back the original EPA administrator William Ruckelshaus, whose tenure Hanley recalled as his "best years" at EPA.

One portion of the administrative state that shrunk under Reagan were the many agency support service workers, whose tasks were privatized, noted Don Kettl, professor of public policy at the University of Maryland. "All the cafeteria, sanitation, maintenance and other blue-collar workers were essentially wrung out of the bureaucracy because of Reagan," he said. "It clearly put people on edge. The paradox is that there were more federal bureaucrats at the end of his administration because of his defense buildup."

Reinventing the State

If there was a hidden cabal of resistant bureaucrats in the 1990s foiling the Clinton administration's far-reaching Reinventing Government campaign, they had a funny way of showing it.

"A lot of the reform ideas came from the bureaucrats we recruited," said Elaine Kamarck, the Brookings Institution scholar who directed the multi-year effort from the White House under Vice President Al Gore. "At one point in 1993, about 2,000 people were working on reinventing government tasks, several hundred of them detailed to the White House, with task forces in every agency," she said.

The "weighty volume of recommendations" the effort produced came out of the career bureaucracy, added Kettl. "A large part of what was celebrated, such as the Hammer Awards for big-impact [reforms], came from leads generated by career officials, seized upon and promoted by Gore."

Some efforts met with resistance, recalled Paul Light. But many in the Clinton administration believed "hardworking feds needed to be liberated from rules." New administrations in both parties often barrel in eager for action, Light said. The difference is that Democrats tend to understand that implementation requires federal employees, he said.

"Federal employees, to their credit, are committed to faithfully executing the laws" no matter what party holds the White House, Light added. "They don't and shouldn't change with each administration."

Kamarck, author of *Why Presidents Fail and How They Can Succeed Again*, said, "Presidents get themselves in trouble by not understanding the bureaucracy." In any organization of two million people, there is something going wrong and something going right at any given time. But even in times of crisis, the mail gets delivered, taxes are collected, Social Security checks go out and customs inspectors protect the borders.

Federal employees follow the law, not the president. If Trump walked into the Agriculture Department and proposed to abandon milk supports, the employees would "probably want selfies with him," she said, but would then say, "Mr. President, thank you very much, but we can't do that, it's against the law."

Trump's Dilemma

Trump experienced a rare moment of bipartisan support in April, when he authorized the launch of 59 cruise missiles into Syria after its government used chemical weapons. He couldn't have done it without an administrative state. "They can criticize the deep state all they want, but why 59 missiles, why that time of day, and why was it aimed at that particular spot in the desert?" asked Kettl. When Trump made a policy decision, "it was executed in a way that only people who knew what they were doing could do it."

The Trump administration's skepticism about the deep state has led to a number of self-inflicted crises and prompted endless discussion about the president's decision-making process. The questions include why he issued a court-blocked travel ban last February without consulting Justice or the Homeland Security Department. Why he tweeted a promise to remove LGBTQ service members from the military without looping in the Pentagon. Why he threatened North Korea with "fire and fury" without a team of foreign policy specialists molding the language.

Ornstein bemoans what he sees as Trump's "war on expertise, war on science," as revealed in his "dismantling" of science advisory panels on the environment. He complains that Secretary of State Rex Tillerson is "driving out some of the best and brightest career diplomats out of sheer incompetence, ignorance, indifference, and hostility."

There's a paradox, added Kettl, in complaining about a deep state and then taking such a long time to make political appointments. While the administration has an ambitious agenda, without appointees in place to implement its plans, it is reliant on career staff to get the work done.

The one area where Trump's staff have demonstrated respect for career employees may be his management agenda with its proposed agency reorganizations to boost efficiency. Budget Director Mick Mulvaney, in tasking agencies to submit reform proposals, has stressed that his team is talking to the Government Accountability Office, the President's Management Council, agency inspectors general as well as countless federal employees. "It is driven by career staff," he told *Government Executive*. "There's no way a political like me from the outside could do it."

Career employees "are the backbone of ensuring that programs are implemented, people are kept safe, and the government performs its role in providing economic opportunity," said Chris Lu, the former deputy Labor secretary. "I probably spent much of my time with budget people and lawyers and information technology experts. The career employees understand a new administration wants to point the ship in a different direction, but they tell you how far you can turn it, how aggressively to move. Listening to them can make the difference in whether or not a policy change is successfully implemented or whether a regulation holds up in court."

The label deep state "assumes there's some kind of planned conspiracy going on," said Devine, the Reagan-era veteran who still bemoans the obstacles to firing federal employees. "It is irrational to allow people to run around government doing anything they want, simply following the parochial interests of their agencies. Federal employees need and legally require political supervision, which was the essence of the Carter reforms, a lesson that the Trump administration Office of Management and Budget needs to explain to the White House rather than promoting a naïve version of the permanent bureaucracy."

EPA alumnus Hanley addressed the deep state by recalling the time doomed EPA Administrator Burford showed up at a retirement party for longtime agency luminary Ed Turk. Having little to fear from the authorities on his last day, Turk told Burford, "Anne, I'll leave you with this thought:

"When Democrats come to Washington, they arrive as an army of liberation. They turn to the civil service and say, 'We love you, go forth and let 1,000 flowers bloom.' Then comes the madness, and the Democrats wake up," Turk said. "Then the Republicans arrive as a conquering army and put their heels on the neck of the civil service. But after about a year or 18 months, they realize that they actually need them to run the place. So they take their heels off the necks, and things are fine."

13

Conspiracy Theories Have a Negative Effect on Our Political System

Joseph E. Uscinski

Joseph E. Uscinski is an American political scientist specializing in the study of conspiracy theories. His most notable work is American Conspiracy Theories, *which he co-authored with Joseph M. Parent.*

Joseph E. Uscinski posits that conspiracy theories of some kind have always been a part of American culture. Such theories came to national attention during the 2016 presidential election, as both candidates were accused of being involved in conspiracy theories. Social scientists have found that people who believe in conspiracy theories tend to view themselves as the victims of a greater power, and Uscinski draws a connection between this tendency and the current political situation in the United States. He asserts that President Trump appealed to people who believe in conspiracy theories because his claims offered them people to blame for their troubles. The internet helps spread conspiracies, but it can also be used to verify claims made by politicians and the media. Uscinski explains why people believe conspiracy theories and how to avoid falling for them.

Conspiracy theories are all about power—who has it and what they are doing with it, particularly when no one is looking.

"The Election Was Rigged, the News Is Fake, and the Deep State Is Out to Get Us," by Joseph E. Uscinski, Eurozine, September 28, 2017. First published in Eurozine as part of the Focal Point "Disinformation and Democracy" (eurozine.com). Reprinted by permission.

The losing side will inevitably accuse those in power of conspiring. Democrats would be convinced that Trump is involved in a grand conspiracy, no matter what evidence was available.

In the last two years, conspiracy theories have become integral to American political discourse. Politicians have shaped priorities and policy around conspiracy claims, and the mainstream media has been all too happy to highlight conspiracy theories in their coverage. Polls show that Americans hold many conspiracy beliefs in the aftermath of the 2016 election. For example, 50 per cent of Democrats believe that Russia hacked the voting machines despite having no evidence of such. That Americans believe in conspiracy theories is nothing new. That conspiracy theories have become so prominent in our political rhetoric is.

Conspiracy theories have always have found a home in the United States. Colonists burned "witches" at the stake, believing they were conspiring with Satan. Early Americans later separated from the British King partially out of concerns of a conspiracy by the crown. A long conspiracy narrative to document this conspiracy is written into the nation's Declaration of Independence. The American Constitution's main feature—separation of powers—is an effort to quell any conspiracy by one branch of government or another.

Since the passage of the Constitution, Americans have imputed conspiracy theories to virtually every group (the British, French, Spanish, Bavarian Illuminati, Freemasons, Slave Power, Abolitionists, Catholics, Jews, Mormons, Muslims, communists and capitalists, to name just a few) and to every major event (assassinations, elections, plane crashes, moon landings and untimely deaths, among many others). Whether we are arguing over major policy issues such as health care, environmental protection, or election integrity, or less important matters such as bicycle sharing programs, conspiracy theories crop up to warn of hidden plots and impending danger. It is difficult to know if the United States is more influenced by conspiracy theories than other nations (social scientists don't yet have enough data to answer this question), but it is enough to say that Americans are no stranger to conspiracy theorizing historically or contemporarily.

More so than any recent election, 2016 was plagued by allegations of schemes and skullduggery. Conspiracy theories became the grounds on which issues were argued and candidates were judged. Either candidates were accused of engaging in far-reaching conspiracies, or they were accused of propagating dubious conspiracy theories. The election's aftermath has seen a continuing wave of conspiracy accusations—mostly surrounding a supposed illicit alliance between Presidents Trump and Putin. These conspiracy theories beget more conspiracy theories and they shape politics and policy.

Most recent accounts of conspiracy theorizing in the media have adopted an alarmist tone—suggesting that Americans have "lost their minds" and that we have entered a "post-truth world." But what is the reality? It is easy to be discouraged by the on-going conspiracy rhetoric, but the social scientists who study conspiracy theories can offer us a very different story—one which, despite the apocalyptic notions of a post-truth world, offers a narrative of stability rather than of impending doom.

When it comes to the amount of conspiracy theorizing plaguing the public, journalists always find it easy to ring the alarm bell. The *New York Times* recently described American politics as "deeply infused with paranoia and distrust." It's easy to be alarmed by such headlines telling of a decent into post-truth conspiracy mania, but when put into context, fears of conspiracy theories are overdrawn and much too frequent. In 2011, the *New York Daily News* declared "It's official: America is becoming a conspiratocracy." Seven years earlier, the *Boston Globe* suggested that 2004 was the "golden age of conspiracy theory." In 1991, the *Washington Post* asserted that we lived "in an age of conspiracy theories," but changed its mind in 1994, when it claimed that Bill Clinton's first term "marked the dawn of a new age of conspiracy theory." In 1977, the *Los Angeles Times* declared that America had hit the high-water mark and were "as conspiracy prone in our judgments as the Pan-Slav nationalists in the 1880s Balkans." I have no idea what was going on in the 1880s Balkans, I can only assume that there were lots of conspiracy theories. Going back to the assassination of JFK, the *New York Times* was sure in 1964 that conspiracy theories had "grown weedlike in this country and abroad."

If the headlines are to be taken seriously, conspiracy theorizing in the US has always been at an all-time high, and is only getting higher. At least 150 per cent of people should be hard-core conspiracy theorists, with daily runs on the grocery store for tin foil. Journalists and commentators in the above instances simply relied on their own impressions without any data or point of comparison. An exploration behind the headlines—into the psychology and politics that drive conspiracy theorizing—might better contextualize the role that conspiracy theories, fake news, and hyper-partisanship are playing in American politics right now.

A Conspiracy Within a Conspiracy: The DNC Leaks

It is true that, in 2016, conspiracy theories became so frequent and at times so bizarre that mainstream news outlets were unsure of how to cover them. For example, Donald Trump's assertion that Senator Ted Cruz's father had taken part in the assassination of JFK in 1963 led the *Washington Post* to proclaim in exasperation, "How on earth is the media supposed to cover Trump's wacky JFK–Cruz conspiracy theory?" While Trump deserves a fair share of the credit for elevating conspiracy theories into the electoral discourse, he can't take all of it. There was fertile ground. And, there were other high-profile politicians trafficking in conspiracy rhetoric.

Political discourse over the last two decades has been riddled with conspiracy theories. Bill Clinton's impeachment was about a vast conspiracy as much as it was about his sexual improprieties. Post 9/11 rhetoric was often driven by conspiracy theories suggesting the Bush Administration murdered thousands of Americans or manufactured pretense for a war just for oil. The

Obama Administration was held in equally low regard: Obama was accused of being a foreign usurper, of blowing up the Deepwater Horizon Well, killing the kids at Sandy Hook, and orchestrating a military take-over of Texas.

Obama's second term was particularly fertile ground for conspiracy theories. 2013 started with a series of scandals involving Benghazi, the wiretapping of journalists and their families, and the IRS targeting of conservative groups. These scandals dragged on through the 2016 campaign and primed the public for an election filled with allegations of fraud, corruption, and cover-ups.

The most prominent conspiracy theory now is that Trump conspired to relieve sanctions if Russia were to help the Trump campaign beat Hillary Clinton. Russia supposedly obliged by hacking into the Democratic National Party's emails. These emails, which painted the DNC in a negative light, were released right before the Democratic convention in which Clinton was to be nominated. The leak mattered because the contents suggested that the Democratic Party rigged the primaries against Bernie Sanders, Clinton's opponent. This of course alienated the more liberal wing of the Democratic Party, perhaps pushing some Sanders supporters to vote for Trump and others to stay home. It became later known that Donna Brazille, who was both a CNN analyst and vice-chair of the DNC, had fed the Clinton campaign debate questions in advance. She initially lied about her role, but was fired and eventually admitted to her wrongdoing. In essence, the Trump conspiracy theories assert that Russia conspired with Trump by exposing an actual conspiracy within the DNC.

The conspiracy theories swirl so fast it is difficult to keep up. During the primaries, Trump was accused of being a Clinton agent whose task was to destroy Republican chances at beating Clinton. Once he won the election, that conspiracy theory went away and was replaced with the theory that Trump conspired with Putin to illicitly win. Trump claimed throughout the campaign that the election would be rigged against him; now he is accused of doing the rigging himself. Immediately after the election, far-left Green Party presidential candidate Jill Stein raised more than seven million dollars, supposedly to investigate irregularities in the voting machines in several states. These irregularities were supposedly the result of Russian hacking. No irregularities were found, and a recount did not ensue. Despite this, Stein is now accused of being a Russian agent.

What Is a Conspiracy Theory?

Just the term "conspiracy theory" has been known to stop fruitful conversations in their tracks. It can imply that an idea is without merit. Beyond this, "conspiracy theory" is often used to refer to a range of concepts—ESP, Bigfoot, Loch Ness Monster, ghosts, aliens, etc.—that go far beyond what I reference here. Let me get the perfunctories out of the way with a brief discussion of what I mean when I say "conspiracy theory."

A "conspiracy" is a small group of powerful persons acting in secret for their own benefit and against the common good. In my usage, conspiracies are large scale assaults on our bedrock institutions and practices. Conspiracies are real and happen all too often. Likely, there are many taking place right now. Prime examples are Richard Nixon's crimes against the Constitution and subsequent cover-up, known as Watergate; the Iran-Contra affair, in which arms were illegally traded for hostages; and the Tuskegee experiments, where doctors injected syphilis into the eyes and spines of African-Americans and Guatemalans without their consent. It is important to acknowledge, however, that just because conspiracies happen, not all conspiracy theories are true.

"Conspiracy theory" refers to an accusation, which may or may not be true, that posits a conspiracy. Conspiracy theories are not concerned with small crimes (e.g. a temptress and her lover devise to kill the cuck husband), but rather with actions that tear at the very fabric of our society. These might include global financial scams, mass brainwashing, depopulation, and interference with democratic institutions and processes. The theory that the CIA killed JFK is a conspiracy theory; so is the notion that climate scientists faked data to precede a socialist take-over. I am obliged to state here—contrary to many conspiracy theorists—that the term "conspiracy theory" was itself not created as part of a CIA conspiracy to hinder scepticism in the aftermath of the Kennedy assassination.

There are millions and millions of conspiracy theories. If you want proof that the internet is not fertile ground for conspiracy theories, just spend a few days on Twitter. Thousands of conspiracy theories will appear each day, but the vast, vast majority will disappear into the night having generated little interest and few followers. It is only a select few that amass a measurable number of believers and any degree of staying power.

Philosophers have invested considerable energy into defining the difference between conspiracies and conspiracy theories. Some of this work focuses on delineating the conspiracy theories which are warranted—those which are likely to be true—from those which are most likely false and should be abandoned. There is a great deal of disagreement on this front, largely because conspiracy theories are non-falsifiable. Given that we expect evidence to be hidden and red-herrings to abound, proving a conspiracy theory true or false is exceptionally difficult. But for the purposes of my usage, the difference between conspiracy and conspiracy theory rest on what is most likely true as determined by our appropriate knowledge-generating institutions. I refer to Watergate as a conspiracy because courts held trials, Congress held hearings, perpetrators went to jail, and the relevant evidence is out in the open for all to see. Theories about JFK's assassination—whether they implicate the CIA, then Vice-President Lyndon Johnson, Cuba, or the Soviet Union—are conspiracy theories because the appropriate institution in this instance, the Warren Commission, determined that one lone assassin, Lee Harvey Oswald, acted on his own and without direction.

Experts, scientists, and officials could be (and are) wrong from time to time, but the best path to truth in those instances is more experts, scientists, and officials rather than more conspiracy theories. Conspiracy theories and theorists can occasionally do good by promoting scepticism and encouraging scrutiny, particularly of the powerful; but as a pathway to truth, conspiracy theories are generally terrible when compared to our mainstream knowledge-generating institutions. Conspiracy theory "methods," if they exist, have never been shown to be reliable.

Nonetheless, if one wants to challenge mainstream wisdom, conspiracy theories are an excellent rhetorical device for doing so. If the evidence is not in one's favour, if one's experts are outnumbered and outmatched, then a conspiracy theory can easily explain away shortcomings and change the grounds of debate. Climate change deniers and creationists typically reach for conspiracy theories to explain why their ideas are not discussed in the mainstream, not included in serious scientific journals, and not endorsed by a consensus of scientists. A conspiracy theory can change the tenor of the debate so that the onus shifts to mainstream scientists and institutions to prove there is no conspiracy, rather on the science deniers whose ideas offer sparse or dubious evidence. In this way, conspiracy theories can act as a disruptive political mechanism.

Much like "conspiracy theory," "conspiracy theorist" is also a freighted term: a few brave souls wear it as a badge, but most would recoil if called one. The term could refer to anyone who believes in a conspiracy theory—which would be every American—or it could be used to refer to a subset of believers, perhaps those who create or propagate conspiracy theories, or those who have a belief system that is comprised largely of conspiracy theories. I favour the latter usage.

How we conceptualize conspiracy theories has a bearing on how we think about them and how we might choose to address them. The conceptual take-away is this: conspiracy theories are dubious ideas that could be true, but probably aren't. Despite this, everyone partakes in conspiracy theorizing from time to time, and some conspiracy theories flourish despite a dearth of evidence. There are two sides to the ledger, of course: sometimes conspiracy theories shed new light on a subject; but usually they leave adherents shadowed in ignorance. If conspiracy theories are so dubious, why do so many people believe them?

People rarely adopt ideas they believe are false. People believe things because they assume those things are true. This is one reason why it is so difficult to discuss religion or politics—people have a set of beliefs and despite any evidence to the contrary, they are convinced those beliefs are correct. Similarly, conspiracy theories often leave little room for negotiation. As much as you might think that beliefs in faked birth certificates, controlled demolitions, or second shooters are unevidenced and irrational, the people that have adopted those beliefs are convinced of their veracity and of their own even-minded evaluation of the "evidence." This matters in democracies: if we are going to call on citizens to make decisions which will be backed by force, then we should want citizens to have the most accurate view of reality possible and to reason as rationally as possible. My research into conspiracy theories suggests that many citizens' views skew far off of reality and that their reasoning is largely biased by socialized worldviews.

Why Do People Believe in Conspiracy Theories?

The most appropriate way to conceive of conspiracy theories is as political opinions. The simplest way to understand how political opinions arise is as the sum of a piece of new information coming in and being laid on top of an existing predisposition that helps us interpret that new information. For example, during the last month of the Obama administration, the final Obama era jobs report came out. The numbers showed national unemployment holding steady at around 4.7 per cent. Democrats looked at the number and thought, "Great job, Obama!" Republicans looked at that same number and thought, "that number isn't picking up on what's really going on out there. And worse, that number may be faked!" Same information, but two very different interpretations.

Election results and party control have an effect on this too. Before Trump won the presidency, Democrats has a very positive view of the economy; Republicans, on the other hand, had a more sour outlook. When Trump was elected, opinions reversed: Democrats began to sour on the economy while Republican views improved dramatically. The economy has not changed much in the last few months, nor has it changed differentially for Democrats than it has for Republicans. In short, our opinions are shaped by our underlying worldviews and suffice it to say it's unwise to assume that our political views are derived from an even-handed assessment of facts.

The most important worldview that drives political opinions in the US is partisanship, and American parties are like tribes. Americans are socialized into having an attachment to a party and once solidified these attachments tend to stick for life. Partisans feel a sense of belonging to their party label and likewise, many also feel a disdain for the opposing party. Once Americans hit middle age, they tend to vote for the same party over and over. So, while campaign coverage in the United States makes it seems as though many Americans are making up their minds about candidates, or switching back and forth between parties, the truth is that because underlying dispositions such as partisanship are stable, partisans' views and behaviours are more stable than the news often lets on. Stories about stability don't attract as many clicks.

Just as a mother would never believe her son a killer, even when presented with fingerprints on the smoking gun, partisans rarely believe their own party has committed a wrong. Partisanship guides the direction that people point their fingers. Republicans believe that Democrats, labour unions, socialists and communists are conspiring. Democrats on the other hand believe that Republicans, corporations, and the wealthy are conspiring. Most of the time, conspiracy theories are just a new mask for old partisan critiques.

Social psychologists converged around the idea that beliefs in specific conspiracy theories tend to derive from a predisposition toward conspiracy logic—I refer to this as conspiracy *thinking*.

Whereas people might believe that they believe a particular conspiracy theory because they think it is true, or at least well-evidenced, social scientists argue that conspiracy beliefs are little more than the conclusions of biased minds. We all have a friend (or worse, family member) who believes every conspiracy theory they encounter—it can't be that this person has stockpiled good evidence for their beliefs, rather it's more likely that they are just predisposed to accept conspiracy theories more so than other explanations.

Perhaps the most important study on the topic shows that conspiracy theorists who believed Princess Diana had been killed by the royal family also believed she was still alive and in hiding; those who believed that Osama bin Laden had been killed before the Navy Seals got to him also believed he was still alive.[1] That conspiracy theorists were willing to believe contradictory narratives suggests that it's not evidence of a particular plot that drives conspiracy theorists, but rather an underlying disposition towards seeing events and circumstances as the product of conspiracy. People that think very strongly in conspiratorial terms need little evidence to suspect a conspiracy—while those who do not think very strongly in conspiratorial terms need much more evidence. Think of this as a continuum rather than a dichotomy: most people are somewhere in the middle. Education and income are good predictors of how much people engage in conspiracy thinking; the poor and uneducated are more likely to think in such terms while the educated and wealthy are less likely to do so.

When we put partisanship and conspiracy thinking together, we end up with a ceiling for partisan conspiracy theories that tops out at about 25 percent. The reason: in order for someone to endorse a partisan conspiracy theory, they must be both inclined to believe in conspiracy theories and be willing to accuse the villain in the particular theory. "Truther" theories that accused the Bush Administration of complicity in the 9/11 terror attacks plateaued at about 25 per cent—Republicans and people resistant to conspiracy logic were not going to believe this theory. The same goes for the "Birther" theory, that Barack Obama faked his birth certificate—this also peaked at around 25 per cent because it could only persuade conspiracy minded Republicans. The good news is that 75 per cent of the country disavows each theory; the bad news is that 50 percent endorsed one of the two.

Conspiracy Theories Are for Losers

Conspiracy theories are, at their core, about power—who has it and what they are doing with it, especially when no one is looking. Conspiracy theories always accuse a villain presumed to be immensely powerful. Rarely do conspiracy theories accuse the powerless, poor, or crippled. It makes perfect sense, then, that if conspiracy theories are about the machinations of the powerful, then conspiracy theorizing would track actual power. The evidence shows this is the case.

When a Republican is in the White House, conspiracy theories tend to accuse Republicans, the wealthy, and corporations; when a Democrat is in the White House, conspiracy theories tend to accuse Democrats, socialists, and communists. We have seen this pendulum swing back and forth with power over the last few decades. During the Bush Administration, Democrats were the ones pushing conspiracy narratives about 9/11, Bush, Cheney, Haliburton, Blackwater, and so on. This switched as soon as Barack Obama won the 2008 election: theories about 9/11 and the "war for oil" became socially inert and were replaced by conspiracy theories about the faked birth certificate and so on. No doubt each of these presidents did things that deserve scrutiny, but the thousands of conspiracy theories that marked their presidencies were well out in front of any evidence. Conspiracy theories are for losers and the losing side is going to accuse those in power of conspiring. It is no shock then that Democrats currently feel cheated and are convinced that Trump is involved in a grand conspiracy. No matter what evidence was available, they would feel this way.

People don't like to be ruled by others. Republicans don't like being ruled by Democrats and vice-versa. People experience anxiety when they are ruled over by others—this is accompanied by the fear that an opposing group can get their way with force. Conspiracy theories help mitigate these fears sort of like a coping mechanism. The weak are in a precarious situation. Victories provide power and resources that breed future victories. To prevent those future victories, out-of-power groups need to revamp and recoup from their losses, close ranks, overcome collective action problems, and sensitize minds to perceived vulnerabilities. Conspiracy theories accomplish these goals by focusing the efforts of the weak toward overcoming the strong.

We see this reflected in our media environment. Because they are in a precarious situation, losers have a need for information; winners don't. Two examples for the cable news market illustrate this. Fox News Channel, which appeals largely to Republicans, achieved very strong ratings following Obama's election in 2008. The Democrats took control of the White House, Senate, and House of Representatives. At the same time, CNN and MSNBC, which appeal to more liberal audiences, faltered. Republicans were under threat and Democrats were not. Fox at the time featured radio host/conspiracy theorist Glenn Beck and his conspiracy chalkboard during their five o'clock spot. When the Republicans took control of the House in 2010, Republican anxiety was at least somewhat tempered; FNC's ratings declined and conspiracy theorist Glenn Beck left the network. We see the opposite now. With Republicans having control of the federal government, MSNBC's ratings have surged, in particular, the viewership for Rachel Maddow's night time program. Maddow has focused her program on Russian conspiracy theories and this has boosted her ratings.

Conspiracy Thinking and the 2016 Presidential Election Campaign

To paint then with broad strokes, Americans believe in conspiracy theories because of dispositional and situational factors. Some people are predisposed because of their socialization to be more accepting of conspiracy theories, and shifts in political power can accentuate those dispositions. Power shifts back and forth in democracies, therefore the prominent conspiracy theories will shift in time to follow that power. This paints a picture of stability more than of change. Why, then, has our information environment been inundated with conspiracy theories and fake news, and why did the American public become so captivated by conspiracy theories during the 2016 election?

The answer to the latter question lies in two candidates, Donald Trump and Bernie Sanders. Both candidates based their campaigns on conspiracy narratives. Trump's frequent conspiracy theories received a lot of notice, but only because he pushed new varieties each week. But, if we were to boil all of his conspiracy theories down into one, it would be this: political elites have sold out the interests of ordinary Americans to foreign interests. Sanders, on the other hand, pushed a single conspiracy theory, that political elites had sold out the interests of ordinary Americans to financial interests, who he referred to as the 1 per cent. Both candidates painted a bleak picture of politics and motivated their crowds with claims of "rigging."

Both Sanders and Trump were "outsider" candidates. Sanders was not really a Democrat; he instead identified during his campaign as a democratic-socialist. This is about as outside as one can get in American politics. Trump was not even a politician and there were many questions about whether his issue positions, if he held any consistently, were congruent with those of the GOP. Sanders was up against Hillary Clinton, who by all accounts was set to be crowned by the Democrats, while Trump was competing against a strong pool of Republican candidates, including Jeb Bush. To justify their existence in the race, each had to turn to conspiracy theories. Why should either party nominate an outsider who is clearly less experienced and less electable than the mainstream choices? This is where Trump's and Sanders' conspiracy theories come in. If the entire process is corrupt, if the experienced political elites are all corrupt, and the media is all corrupt, then experience, endorsements, and mainstream views should count for nothing.

Given that Trump and Sanders appealed to the conspiracy-minded members of their respective parties, it is no surprise then that each of them received about 40 per cent of the votes during the primaries. For Trump, this plurality was enough to win the nomination, because the field of mainstream candidates opposing him divided the mainstream vote.

Normally, politicians who espouse conspiracy theories do not get far in America. They could make a short-term splash, like Senator Joseph McCarthy, but they tend to face ridicule and fade away rather quickly. The mainstream media—with some exceptions—is quick to denounce politicians who push conspiracy theories. Trump and Sanders were able to prosper with conspiracy theories for two different reasons. Trump was able to excite a sector of voters who felt underrepresented by the mainstream GOP, and he was able to mobilize new voters because his mix of conspiracy theories and nationalism resonated with them. Sanders was able to mobilize the conspiracy-minded left wing of the Democratic Party because he appealed to its belief that the system was rigged against it by a small group of high earners. In short, conspiracy-minded people exist in each party and have been underserved by party rhetoric in the past. Trump and Sanders gave these conspiracy-minded people what they wanted. It isn't so much that demands changed, it's just that Trump and Sanders both made bold attempts to capitalize on it. The same logic applies to the current "epidemic" of fake news plaguing our information environment.

Time to Start Worrying?

It is true the false ideas plague our political discourse. Some of these ideas are shared widely on social media, so much so that they sometimes outshine more accurate news. Should we be concerned? The short answer is no. Fake and frauds have always existed; the fact we are noticing them more now is a testament to our concern over truth, rather than our disdain for it.

Fakes news can spread fast. Conspiracy theories, in particular, have found a home on the internet and can be shared easily on social media, sometimes creating a wildfire of false beliefs. During the election, fake headlines—for example, those claiming Hillary Clinton was dead—were shared despite having no truth to them. The assumption is that these false ideas pop up on social media and are shared indiscriminately by users. This makes a good headline of course, but contrary to most of the claims made by journalists and commenters, this is not the case. People who are resistant to conspiracy theories won't traffic in them on the internet, and partisans won't traffic in conspiracy theories that accuse co-partisans. This leaves the online conspiracy theorizing to those who believe in conspiracy theories anyway.

The bigger picture is that while there are conspiracy theories on the internet, we have overestimated their place there. Everything—recipes, kitten videos, sports—is on the internet, yet it seems that we only think that conspiracy theories and other forms of dubious information are taking over. To put this idea to rest, consider the following. There is currently no evidence to suggest that public beliefs in conspiracy theories have increased since the internet or social media were rolled out. Most conspiracy theories that arise on the internet die on the vine. The websites that traffic in conspiracy theories do not get anywhere near the amount of web traffic that mainstream websites do. People go to the internet to get real news, book travel, get dates, and look at porn in far higher numbers than they go to look at conspiracy theories.

There are good reasons to suspect that the internet has tamed conspiracy theories and false information. First, the internet and social media provide easy access to authoritative sources. People don't need to rely on village wisdom to solve problems, they can get immediate authoritative information at the touch of a button. But more importantly, peoples' dispositions still drive what they believe, and elites still largely drive the contours of public opinion. There just isn't enough room for fake news to affect anyone who doesn't already have a worldview driven toward dubious ideas to begin with.

For fear of upending a great narrative, fears of a post-truth world are vastly overblown. First, if we had descended into a post-truth world, we probably would not know it, nor would anyone care. The fact that we are having a conversation about the accuracy of our information environment is proof—to a certain extent—that we do care about truth.

References
Wood, M., et al. (2012). "Dead and Alive: Beliefs in Contradictory Conspiracy Theories." *Social Psychological and Personality Science* 3(6): 767-773.

Organizations to Contact

The editors have compiled the following list of organizations concerned with the issues debated in this book. The descriptions are derived from materials provided by the organizations. All have publications or information available for interested readers. The list was compiled on the date of publication of the present volume; the information provided here may change. Be aware that many organizations take several weeks or longer to respond to inquiries, so allow as much time as possible.

The American Council of Young Political Leaders
1030 15th Street NW
Suite 580 West
Washington, DC 20005
(202) 857-0999
website: http://acypl.org

The ACYPL is a nonpartisan nonprofit organization that seeks to introduce future political and policy leaders to international affairs. It promotes mutual understanding and respect through establishing programs with strategically important countries, nascent democracies, and longtime allies, facilitating exchange programs with these countries. It also conducts multinational programs on topics of global or regional importance. Since its founding, ACYPL has worked in 121 countries.

Central Intelligence Agency
Office of Public Affairs
Washington, DC 20505
(703) 482-0623
website: www.cia.gov/index.html

The CIA preempts national security threats and furthers security objectives by collecting intelligence, using this information to provide tactical and strategic advantage for the United States. It collects and evaluates foreign intelligence to assist the president and government policymakers in making decisions regarding national security, but it does not actively take place in policymaking.

Envision
1919 Gallows Road
Suite 700
Vienna, VA 22182
(703) 584-9380
email: envisioninfo@envisionexperience.com
website: www.envisionexperience.com

Envision offers career, leadership, and technological programs to help students make their political career aspirations a reality. It offers political educational programs in Washington, DC, as well as countries around the world, to equip young people for careers in national security, international relations, and other forms of political leadership.

The Freechild Institute
PO Box 6185
Olympia, WA 98507-6185
(360) 489-9680
email: info@freechild.org
website: www.freechild.org

The Freechild program endeavors to politically empower young adults and allow them to engage in social change. It encourages activism and provides young people the tools they need to effectively engage in it. Freechild also consults with nonprofits and government agencies and trains youth and adult leaders to promote political engagement among young adults, ensuring that regardless of the political issue at hand, young people will be able to have a voice in it.

National Scholastic Press Association
2829 University Avenue SE, Suite 720
Minneapolis, MN 55414
(612) 200-9254
email: info@studentpress.org
website: http://studentpress.org

The National Scholastic Press Association is a nonprofit educational service dedicated to providing journalism education sources. It utilizes education training and recognition programs for members to promote the standards and ethics of good journalism as accepted and practiced by print, broadcast, and electronic media in the United States.

The National Whistleblower Center
PO Box 25074
Washington, DC 20027
(202) 342-1903
email: contact@whistleblowers.org
website: www.whistleblowers.org

The NWC is the leading nonprofit in whistleblower legal advocacy. It is a nonpartisan organization that provides advocacy and services on behalf of whistleblowers, including advocating for the improvement of whistleblower protections, providing legal referrals to whistleblowers in need of legal counsel, and drafting and supporting various important pieces of whistleblower legislation.

Project Looksharp
1119 Williams Hall
Ithaca, NY 14850-7290
(607) 274-3471
email: looksharp@ithaca.edu
website: www.projectlooksharp.org

Project Looksharp is a media literacy organization run by Ithaca College. It works with educators by providing lesson plans, media materials, training, and support for the integration of media literacy into classroom curricula. Part of Project Looksharp's curriculum involves teaching students how to evaluate news articles.

Public Citizen
1600 20th Street NW
Washington, DC 20009
(202) 588-1000
email: member@citizen.org
website: www.citizen.org

Founded in 1971, Public Citizen is a nonprofit organization that lobbies for the interests of citizens. It does not endorse candidates for political office. It has challenged the practices of the pharmaceutical, nuclear, and automobile industries and attacked what it perceives to be undemocratic trade agreements before Congress, executive branch agencies, and the judicial system.

The Student Press Law Center
1608 Rhode Island Avenue NW
Suite 211
Washington, DC 20036
(202) 785-5450
email: splc@splc.org
website: www.splc.org

The Student Press Law Center is a nonprofit, nonpartisan corporation that provides free legal advice and educational tools to student journalists. It is the only legal assistance agency devoted exclusively to educating high school and college journalists about their First Amendment rights and responsibilities and supporting student news media from censorship. It also provides free legal representation to student journalists when necessary.

US Securities and Exchange Commission
100 F Street NE
Washington, DC 20549
(202) 551-2100
email: chairmanoffice@sec.gov
website: www.sec.gov

The SEC is a federal agency that works to protect the interests of all investors. It works to maintain fair and functional markets through regulation. The SEC oversees securities exchanges, brokers and dealers, investment advisers, and mutual funds to ensure that all investors have access to certain basic facts about an investment prior to buying it and while they hold it. It endeavors to ensure transparency in the capital market.

Bibliography

Books

Marc Ambinder and D. B. Grady. *Deep State: Inside the Government Secrecy Industry*. New York, NY: Wiley, 2013.

Rob Brotherton. *Suspicious Minds: Why We Believe Conspiracy Theories*. New York, NY: Bloomsbury Sigma, 2017.

Tom Engelhardt. *Shadow Government: Surveillance, Secret Wars, and a Global Security State in a Single-Superpower World*. New York, NY: Haymarket Books, 2014.

Glenn Greenwald. *No Place to Hide: Edward Snowden, the NSA, and the U.S. Surveillance State*. New York, NY: Picador, 2015.

Michael V. Hayden. *Playing to the Edge: American Intelligence in the Age of Terror*. New York, NY: Penguin, 2017.

Mike Lofgren. *The Deep State: The Fall of the Constitution and the Rise of a Shadow Government*. New York, NY: Penguin, 2016.

Jane Mayer. *Dark Money: The Hidden History of the Billionaires Behind the Rise of the Radical Right*. New York, NY: Anchor, 2017.

Peter Dale Scott. *The American Deep State: Big Money, Big Oil, and the Struggle for U.S. Democracy*. Lanham, MD: Rowman & Littlefield, 2017.

David Talbot. *The Devil's Chessboard: Allen Dulles, the CIA, and the Rise of America's Secret Government*. New York, NY: Harper Perennial, 2017.

Douglas Valentine. *The CIA as Organized Crime: How Illegal Operations Corrupt America and the World*. Atlanta, GA: Clarity Press, 2017.

Periodicals and Internet Sources

Matthew Cole and Jeremy Scahill, "Trump White House Weighing Plans for Private Spies to Counter 'Deep State' Enemies," *Intercept*, December 4, 2017. https://theintercept .com/2017/12/04/trump-white-house-weighing-plans-for -private-spies-to-counter-deep-state-enemies.

Michael Crowley, "The Deep State Is Real," *Politico*, September 2017. https://www.politico.com/magazine/story/2017 /09/05/deep-state-real-cia-fbi-intelligence-215537.

Dexter Filkins, "The Deep State," *New Yorker*, March 12, 2012. https://www.newyorker.com/magazine/2012/03/12/the -deep-state.

David A. Graham, "There Is No American 'Deep State,'" *Atlantic*, February 20, 2017. https://www.theatlantic.com /international/archive/2017/02/why-its-dangerous-to-talk -about-a-deep-state/517221.

Greg Grandin, "What Is the Deep State?" *Nation*, February 17, 2017. https://www.thenation.com/article/what-is-the-deep -state.

Mike Lofgren, "Essay: Anatomy of the Deep State," *Bill Moyers*, Feb 21, 2014, http://billmoyers.com/2014/02/21/anatomy- of-the-deep-state.

Jon D. Michaels, "Trump and the 'Deep State,'" *Foreign Affairs*, September/October 2017. https://www.foreignaffairs.com /articles/2017-08-15/trump-and-deep-state.

Mikel Ofgren, "Yes, There Is a Deep State—But Not the Right Wing's Caricature," Mikel Ofgren, March 16, 2017. https:// www.mikelofgren.net/yes-there-is-a-deep-state-but-not -the-right-wings-caricature.

Abigale Tracy, "'It Is Foreboding': Inside the Deep State, Dina Powell's Departure Looks Like an Omen," *Vanity Fair,* December 8, 2017. https://www.vanityfair.com /news/2017/12/dina-powell-deputy-national-security-adviser-white-house.

Z. Byron Wolf, "Trump Embraces Deep State Conspiracy Theory," *CNN Politics,* November 29, 2017. http://www.cnn .com/2017/11/29/politics/donald-trump-deep-state/index .html.

Index

V

W